W9-BKC-659

The **Plank Grilling Cookbook**

THE
PLANK GRILLING
COOKBOOK

INFUSE FOOD *with* **MORE FLAVOR** *using* WOOD PLANKS

Dina Guillen
Michelle Lowrey
Maria Everly
Gretchen Bernsdorff

Photographs by Diane Padys

SASQUATCH BOOKS
SEATTLE

Copyright ©2006 by Dina Guillen, Michelle Lowrey, Maria Everly, and
    Gretchen Bernsdorff
Photography copyright ©2006 by Diane Padys, L'Image Magick, Inc.

All rights reserved. No portion of this book may be reproduced or utilized
in any form, or by any electronic, mechanical, or other means without the
prior written permission of the publisher.

Printed in Canada
Published by Sasquatch Books
Distributed by Publishers Group West
13 12 11 10 09 08   9 8 7 6 5

The photographer would like to thank Rob & Tara Albrecht
for making their beautiful home by the lake available.
Thank you, especially, Patty, for the generous access to your gorgeous
garden, and for making the food look so delicious.

Cover/Interior Design and Composition: Stewart A. Williams
Cover Design (ISBN 1-57061-528-4): Liza Brice-Dahmen
Food Styling: Patty Wittmann
Prop Styling: Cynthia Verner
Photograph of the authors: Kyle B. Thompson

Library of Congress Cataloging-in-Publication Data
The plank grilling cookbook : infuse food with more flavor using wood
planks / by Dina Guillen . . . [et al.].
p. cm.
ISBN 1-57061-474-1 (black text version)
ISBN 1-57061-528-4 (brown text version, SKU 9053729)
1. Barbecue cookery. 2. Wood. I. Guillen, Dina.

TX840.B3P58 2006
641.5'784--dc22

                                                    2005057850

Sasquatch Books
119 South Main Street, Suite 400
Seattle, WA 98104
(206) 467-4300
www.sasquatchbooks.com
custserv@sasquatchbooks.com

This book is dedicated to Sam Nassar *and*
in memory of Anna Curtis. We love you.

Contents

Introduction

If you have gone so far as to buy this cookbook, you no doubt are intrigued by the prospect of plank grilling. If you are anything like the four of us, you picked up a nicely packaged set of planks, with visions of all the culinary delights you would prepare with them, only to realize you have absolutely no idea what to do with them now that you have gotten them home. We are here to tell you that you are not alone.

We are members of a nearly five-year-old cooking club that meets once a month to try different cuisines and learn new cooking techniques. Maria and Michelle are the original founders. It all started when Maria hosted a summer barbecue. Maria was sharing that she belonged to a cooking club that was thoroughly enjoyable, yet she found herself inexplicably cheating on recipes. All the recipes were light and healthy—food styles that Maria prescribes to on a daily basis—but she found herself wanting to stretch the bounds of culinary techniques and ingredients during her cooking club gatherings. When the recipe called for skim milk, Maria would find herself adding cream just to create a richer dish. When the recipe called for "mixing," Maria would "emulsify," just to learn the technique.

Michelle, who had recently left her job as a pastry chef to become a stay-at-home mom, was approached by Maria who suggested they create a "gourmet" cooking club. They met at a local restaurant to discuss the idea with friends. These were friends who love to cook, love to eat, and love to laugh at themselves (a necessity when you don't know what you are doing when preparing gourmet meals). Thus, while at the restaurant drinking lemon drop martinis, the Lemon Drops Cooking Club was formed.

Once a month a rotating host sends out a beautiful invitation to each member, enclosing the menu and a recipe to be prepared and brought. The host always prepares the entrée, and the rest of us bring the appetizers, soups, salads, side dishes, and desserts.

The club was touch and go at first. Friends would join for the wonderful camaraderie and the good food, but would leave after a few months when asked to bake their first soufflé. We were trying to make everything, from homemade bacon to homemade ice cream, oftentimes resulting in a fiery and slushy mess. Ultimately a consistent group formed, made up of women with a passion for cooking (and who could not be embarrassed nor deterred easily). The renamed Kitchen Table Cooking Club came to life.

This once-a-month event is sacred. There is something immensely satisfying about coming together for a meal prepared by our hands. Not only do we share our immense passion for food, we share a united feeling of sisterhood that lasts us until the next meeting. Cooking club is where we say good-bye to our small children for a couple of hours, leave the responsibilities of work at the office, and enjoy dear friends. We share our hopes and dreams for the future, cry a little, and laugh a lot. Funny what you can learn about someone over a perfect glass of Bordeaux.

When Dina was first invited to join the club, Michelle warned her with these haunting words: "We don't do tacos." To this day, every time it's Dina's turn to host, those words come to her mind when she prepares her menu. Nowadays, she is not so intimidated, but back when she first joined the group those words shook her to the bone. Her need to impress inspired her to telephone her brother, Sam, who sold baking and grilling planks. Dina asked him to send her some grilling planks that she could use to prepare her next cooking club entrée.

Since there weren't any plank grilling recipes (other than for salmon) or plank grilling cookbooks on the market, Dina searched for a recipe that she could easily convert to the method. She chose a pan-roasted quail with port sauce that sounded wonderful, and instead of pan roasting she was going to try grilling them on the plank. With no clue about how to use the plank, she practiced for weeks prior to cooking club to ensure a fire-free gathering.

The appointed day arrived and we all headed for Dina's house. She had set a few planks on her kitchen island, and one by one we picked them up to investigate. We were very unimpressed with these pieces of wood. Michelle at one point asked Dina if they were "glorified roof shingles."

As Dina started heating the planks on the barbecue, our curiosity began to pique. She placed the quails on the heated planks, closed the lid, and delicious smoke began to emanate from the grill. The lowly grilling plank now had everyone's attention. As Dina removed the food from the grill, we all noticed the beautiful mahogany glaze that had formed on the quail and the mouthwatering aroma filling the air. This smoke- and wood-infused dish was nothing short of spectacular. We knew we had something very special on our hands. Using the grilling plank was the start of a great culinary adventure that would lead us to this cookbook.

We all have horror stories from our first plank grilling experiences (all except Maria, who never burned a plank while creating this cookbook). On one of Gretchen's turns to host, she was happily scurrying around cleaning, cooking, lighting candles, and getting the mood set. As we were gathering, Gretchen noticed Dina and Michelle looking out onto the patio. They both started snickering. She looked at them and decided she must be missing out on some juicy details and had to investigate. Actually, Gretchen's latest plank grilling experience was the juicy detail. She had neglected to discard the evidence from her latest disaster, and there on her patio were the charred, brittle remains of a plank. No need for explanations. We just started laughing.

Michelle remembers the first time she tried to grill some fish on a plank. She had seen it done on television countless times. "Piece of cake," she thought. "I'll just slap this piece of salmon onto this glorified shingle, and, presto, dinner is served." Well, that is not exactly how things turned out. The next thing she remembers, there looked to be a small brush fire belching forth from her grill in all its glory. Stunned, she quickly grabbed some pot holders and flung the burning plank across the patio, salmon steak and all. She grabbed the garden hose and put the fire out, with the kids screaming in the background, "Mommy, do it again!" While she loves to entertain her children, flaming salmon flying through the air is not anyone's idea of fun. In a fiery instant, her thoughts of overtaking her husband as "The Grill Master" were dashed. She quickly cleaned up the mess, hid the evidence, and told her husband they were going out for pizza.

Now, let us tell you, all four of us love to cook. We live for that next great meal. We know our way around the kitchen, so what happened? What happened was that none of us could find an in-depth set of instructions or a cookbook to tell us how to plank-grill.

We did, however, have one invaluable source: Dina's brother, Sam Nassar. Sam is the owner of a plank distributor in Seattle, Washington. Over the years, he has heard about our cooking club exploits and the many adventures we have embarked on trying new foods, cooking gadgets, and culinary techniques. When he heard that we were interested in learning more about plank grilling, he gave us advice and tips and guidance throughout the process.

Along the way, Sam asked us to consider writing recipes and even a cookbook about plank grilling once we became proficient at the technique. He was intrigued by the idea that a group of nonprofessional cooks could convey the ease and joy of plank grilling. Many people incorrectly considered plank grilling the exclusive domain of professional chefs. Recipes by a cooking club would be a great way to dispel that perception.

Sam was wonderful (read patient) in answering our questions, and he loved that we were so intrigued by this style of cooking. It is because of Sam Nassar that this cookbook exists, and we thank him from the bottom of our hearts for planting the seed, as well as for supplying grilling planks so we could run with his idea of writing a cookbook.

But could we do this? Why not? There was certainly a need for this type of cookbook. That we are women did give us some pause, though. Women writing a book about grilling? It's just not done! We thought for sure there were laws on the books somewhere preventing us from treading on the hallowed grounds of men and their precious barbecues. Since the dawn of time, men have bowed to the altar of fire. They are fascinated by all things that burn, something we had never understood.

Well, after the countless hours over our backyard barbecues, we now can say that we get it. We truly get it. Grilling is fun! We thought by having our husbands man the grill we were getting them out of our hair for a while. Turns out they were having all the fun.

Plank grilling has really changed the way we all think about traditional grilling. The first few times we tried grilling on the plank it was out of curiosity. These days we would not think of grilling anything any other way. I guess you could say the plank has spoiled us. Gone are the days of overcooked, dry poultry and pork chops. And steaks that are burnt on the outside and raw in the middle are luckily part of our culinary pasts.

Plank grilling gives your food the flavor of a smoker with the convenience of a grill. There are so many people that love the taste of smoked foods but don't want to invest the time needed to smoke foods in a smoker. With plank grilling, that smoky flavor is achieved in the same amount of time required to grill, with the added bonus of the food being flavored with the scent of wood. Until you have tried it, you cannot imagine how amazing food tastes once it has been infused with wood and smoke.

Another great aspect of the plank is the way it retains moisture in foods. One of the first things you'll notice when plank-grilling is how juicy and moist the food tastes. A soaked plank moistens the heat while shielding food from direct flames, allowing foods like meats to grill in their own juices on a flat surface instead of the juice dripping through the grill grate and evaporating.

The days of charring larger cuts of meat when grilling are over too. Like we said earlier, instead of overcooking the outside and undercooking the inside as a result of exposing thicker or larger cuts of meat to direct flame, the plank buffers the heat and allows the barbecue to operate like an oven.

Lastly, everything that comes off the plank is beautiful in presentation. The smoke gives food a rich caramelized color. To make the presentation even more special, serve foods directly from the plank. It will turn an everyday dish into something that ignites your senses.

Every recipe in this cookbook was created and tested by us and consumed by our wonderful families, friends, and neighbors. Since having embarked on this culinary journey, we have created some amazing recipes, started (and extinguished) more than three hundred fires, formed lifelong friendships, and have had way more fun than should be allowed. We invite you to give this way of grilling a try. You will be amazed at how great the food tastes.

Through this cookbook, we hope you gather together your newfound knowledge of plank grilling and share it with your family and friends as we have. Food is most certainly love, and we hope that the love we have for this book, and each other, shines through on every page you read and in every delicious bite you eat. *Salut*!

History *of* Plank Grilling

Plank grilling represents a part of our early heritage, when spirit, nature, and food were all celebrated as one. This book pays tribute to this generations-old tradition of cooking, popularly practiced among American Indians centuries ago. The cuisine incorporated sides of fish split down the middle that were then bound and secured to driftwood and cooked vertically, downwind of a roaring fire. Not only did American Indians season their food with the aromatic woodsmoke, giving it an amazing taste and flavor, but also the food they cooked over wood stayed moist all the way through since it grilled in its own juices.

Alder and cedar were the most common types of wood used by American Indian tribes of the Pacific Northwest. In fact, legend has it that there are healing powers in cooking with cedar. And if you have ever tasted food grilled on cedar, you will understand why this traditional method has endured for centuries.

Many fine restaurants and gourmet chefs around the country now recognize plank grilling as a wonderful culinary technique. Seastar Restaurant and Raw Bar in Bellevue, Washington, offers plank-grilled appetizers and entrées, including mushrooms, salmon, and Alaskan king crab, each roasted on cedar planks.

Spenger's Fish Grotto in Berkeley, California, and District Chophouse and Brewery in Washington DC both offer cedar-plank-grilled salmon. Angels Restaurant in New York has plank-grilled and roasted vegetable sandwiches (just the vegetables are grilled, not the entire sandwich). Shaw's Crab House in Chicago serves plank-grilled Lake Superior whitefish with duchesse potatoes. And Ruffino's restaurant in Baton Rouge, Lousiana, serves up a cedar-plank-baked redfish.

The nation's finest restaurants have inspired many backyard chefs to bring this fascinating, unique, and delicious culinary technique to America's dinner tables. We hope our cookbook encourages and motivates more home cooks to try plank grilling. Whatever type of wood you use, what you create will be among the best-tasting and juiciest meals you have ever prepared.

Types *of* **Planks: Characteristics, Flavors,** *and* **Pairings**

Wood-plank grilling is an alternative cooking method to the traditional barbecue grill. Wood planks give off a smoky, woodsy aroma, and the result is food that is more moist, healthy, and flavorful. In addition, your food will be infused with a subtle smokiness without overpowering and overwhelming other flavors.

A major plus to this cooking technique is that wood planks are extremely easy and fun to use. In addition, the look and presentation of the final dish are so beautiful that a photograph is warranted. Finally, since plank grilling requires little supervision, you can spend more time socializing and enjoying yourself. What can be better than that!

Wood planks come in different shapes, sizes, and thicknesses and typically come prepackaged in sets of three or four. Sized to fit standard grills, planks are available at most cookware stores, specialty stores, seafood markets, and on the Internet. Wood planks typically come in two forms: grilling planks and baking planks. Grilling planks are approximately ⅜ inch thick, are limited to one to four uses, and are primarily for gas- or charcoal-grill applications. Baking planks are made for oven use and can be used indefinitely if taken care of properly. This cookbook focuses exclusively on grilling planks.

The various types of wood planks available include alder, cedar, cherry, hickory, maple, and oak. We do not recommend you use woods such as pine, birch, or fir because they impart a harsh flavor. The flavors of individual woods are often very subtle, which is why most of our recipes can be created on any type of wood listed below, unless noted otherwise in the recipe. Alder and cedar are the most popular and most common types of planks found in the marketplace.

ALDER: Gives a mild flavor with a light touch that finely accents all foods. Great with seafood, beef, pork, poultry, duck, fruit, vegetables, herbs, nuts, spices, and breads. Alder and butter go together like peanut butter and jelly.

CEDAR: This is the most flavor-inducing and aromatic of all the woods. The flavor can be intense and permeates very well without being overpowering. Cedar is the best complement to salmon. Cedar also pairs nicely with any other fish, seafood, pork, chicken, vegetables, and fruit. Spicy foods are an excellent choice with this type of plank, as are sauces, sautés, and glazes with a high sugar content, such as maple syrup, molasses, and fruit preserves. Fruit-based desserts, such as

Pecan and Cinnamon Stuffed Apples with Caramel Sauce (page 132), *Pineapple Sundaes* (page 134), and *Peaches with Crème Fraîche Topping* (page 129), are also great choices.

CHERRY: Rich in flavor, cherry planks can be used with a variety of foods, including all meats, and are highly recommended for desserts. As with oak, cherry can be a bit acidic. Bananas, peaches, and all berries are particularly great when prepared on cherrywood. Cherry planks are not as readily available as the other wood types. Hunt around in specialty stores or visit Internet sites.

HICKORY: Offers a strong smoky flavor. Good with beef, pork, and chicken, and great with dishes using highly seasoned rubs and sauces.

MAPLE: Imparts a mild, sweet, and smoky flavor that pairs well with all types of beef, bacon, duck, lamb, venison, and fruits. Dishes using highly seasoned rubs and sauces are also great, particularly when paired with red wine.

OAK: With a moderate to high acidity without being bitter, an oak plank imparts a flavor similar to the oak flavor found in chardonnay. Fruits, nuts, butter, vanilla, and cinnamon complement this type of wood quite well. Oak is also excellent with fish, pork, turkey, chicken, game birds, lamb, liver, rabbit, veal, beef, and breads. As with cherry planks, you may have to shop around to locate oak planks.

The type of plank you ultimately choose will be based largely on personal preference. When deciding, think of the strength of the flavor you want to come across in your food. What other foods or side dishes are you serving and what type of beverages? Decide if you want to complement or contrast those flavors.

Being foodies, we like to think plank pairing is similar to wine pairing. Pairing wine with food is an art form. However, personal preferences ultimately dictate what wine, food, and plank go best together. We offer suggestions, but you will be much happier following your own path. So be a rebel and feel free to break the rules. You do not have to pair white wines with fish and seafood or red wines with red meat. Similarly, you do not have to grill salmon on a cedar plank. It's your grill; you make and break the rules.

Learning *the* Art *of* Plank Grilling

Needless to say there is a learning curve and an art to plank grilling. Do not be discouraged if you ignite a few planks during the process of perfecting your skills. Each of us has seen flames spewing out of our grills and had to resort to turning the garden hose into a fire hose. A few pearls of wisdom and some general guidelines will help make you an artisan in the craft of plank grilling.

An important note before beginning your culinary journey into plank grilling: We have experimented with both gas grills and charcoal grills with our planks. Gas grills, by far, are the preferred tool, since consistent cooking temperatures are essential. As a result, our tips, guidelines, and recipes are all customized for gas grills.

That is not to say, however, that charcoal grills cannot be used with plank grilling. If that is what you have, then by all means, throw a plank on the barbie and enjoy the rich smoky flavors of plank grilling. You will, however, need to monitor your grill a lot more closely during the cooking time and pay close attention to flare-ups.

Plank Preparation *and* Grilling

Soaking the Plank

Prior to using your plank on the grill, it should be soaked to increase moisture, resist burning, and extend the life of the plank. The longer the plank is soaked, the better the results. Soaking time can be shortened by using hot water.

TO SOAK THE PLANK:

1. Begin by rinsing the plank.

2. Fill the kitchen sink, a large basin, or other container large enough to fit the plank into with water.

3. Submerge the entire plank in water, placing a weight on it to prevent it from floating to the top. Soak in water for at least 1 hour and up to 24 hours. Allowing more moisture to soak into the plank diminishes the risk of burning it as well as produces the maximum amount of smoke.

4. To enhance the flavors imparted by the plank, add approximately 1 table-spoon of salt to the water. Additional flavor modifications can be achieved by adding apple cider vinegar, white wine vinegar, dry white wine, citrus, flavored liquors, or berry juice to the water.

Preheating the Plank

After the plank has been soaked it must be preheated, similar to preheating an oven prior to baking. There are a few reasons for this. First, preheating the plank controls the amount of warping. Second, a lightly charred wood allows optimal flavor to permeate the food cooked on the plank. Third, preheating the plank will provide you with a sterilized wood surface on which to place the food. Allowing the food to have direct contact with the wood is optimal for the maximum amount of flavor infusion.

TO PREHEAT THE PLANK:

1. Start by preheating your grill according to the manufacturer's instructions.

2. Bring your grill temperature to a medium-high heat, approximately 425 degrees F. Then place the plank on the grill and close the grill's lid.

3. Plank placement on the grill is important. A plank placed at the proper height will allow the most control for preventing flare-ups or burning. The plank should be approximately 8 inches away from the flame. If you do not have control over the plank height, closely monitor the grill during preheating and cooking.

4. The plank will begin to smoke lightly. You may hear some crackling and popping as the plank begins to bow and flex.

5. After 3 to 5 minutes the plank will be lightly charred on one side and possibly bowed. Open the grill, flip the plank over, and reclose the grill lid. A heat-seasoned plank controls warping, so carefully flip and toast each side of the plank a few times, 1 to 2 minutes per side, until the plank flattens out.

6. Use plank immediately after preheating.

Grilling Food on the Plank

The secret to perfectly plank-grilled food is the smoke. Once the grill lid has been closed, the color and density of the smoke will be your guide. You may need to hang around the grill and adjust the flame to get that "just right" consistent-looking smoke. And we cannot say it enough: Resist the temptation to open the grill. It will make all the difference.

TO GRILL FOOD ON THE PLANK:

1. Pick the best side of the plank and place the food directly on the plank. The best side of the plank will be lightly charred, which imparts better flavor. The plank should also be flat or bowed slightly upward. A flat plank captures the juices as the food cooks and retains moisture.

2. Unless noted otherwise in a recipe, food placement on the plank should be in a single layer. In addition to the smoke, contact with the wood allows flavor to infuse the food.

3. Once you have placed the plank and food on the grill, close the lid and let the magic begin. You will find that our recipes do not stipulate grilling temperature. Concentrate on the look of the smoke to determine the proper temperature. Monitor the smoke in terms of its denseness, color, and consistency of stream. (See Monitoring the Smoke below.)

4. Plank grilling is similar to oven heating, cooking from all sides; therefore, food does not need to be flipped or turned over unless the recipe specifically states to do so.

Monitoring the Smoke

Plank grilling is all about smoke. Finding the right amount of heat to guarantee a slow and steady stream of smoke during the entire grilling time is one of the most important steps to master. You do not want too much smoke, because the plank will catch on fire. Conversely, you do not want too little smoke, because smoke is needed to surround the food and infuse it with incredible flavor. The moisture in the smoke also keeps food from drying as it cooks.

You want to see a constant flow of light gray to white smoke coming out of your barbecue throughout the entire cooking time. You may need to adjust the heat during grilling to achieve the desired steady flow of smoke. If the smoke begins to become moderately heavy, turn the heat down to a lower setting. *The smoke should not diminish completely but should become lightly visible and steady.*

With some grills, especially charcoal grills or gas grills that do not have multiple levels of racks, it can be difficult to get a light smoke. The results will still be flavorful, but keep a vigilant watch for flames.

When plank grilling, a very important note of caution: The constant tendrils of smoke that emanate from your grill may be giving your food wonderful flavor, but not your clothing and hair! The smoke can penetrate into your clothes and hair, making them smell like a small brush fire. If you need to protect your clothing, you can wear a smock. A large oversized shirt serves well for this purpose. Look like a true pro and wear a chef's hat to protect your hair.

Timing of Soaking the Plank, Food Preparation, and Preheating the Plank

In order to fully master the art of plank grilling, it is helpful to consider the timing of events. Plank grilling, while easy, involves several key steps that require the coordination of timing soaking the plank, preparing the food, and preheating the plank. To become familiar with the process follow these tips for timing:

1. Read the recipe in its entirety to determine how long it will take to prep food for plank grilling. For example, pay attention to food preparation instructions that require foods to be marinated for several hours or overnight.

2. Before preparing each recipe, the first step should always be soaking the plank. If food preparation calls for an overnight marinade, go ahead and soak your plank before beginning the prepping of the marinade. It is better to soak your plank overnight versus forgetting to soak your plank at all.

3. Continue soaking the plank until the food is ready to grill. Once food preparation has been completed, remove the plank from the water and preheat it.

4. Immediately upon preheating the plank, place the food directly on the plank and begin grilling. The plank should go directly from soaking, to preheating, to grilling without a lapse in time between each step.

Reusing the Plank

To make the most of your plank, it can be reused approximately two to four times. This will depend upon the thickness of the plank and the length of grilling time from prior uses. Eventually, the plank will reach a peak and will need to be discarded. You do not have to trash the plank entirely, though. You can simply crumble the plank into pieces and toss them into the charcoal as seasoning chips.

TO REUSE THE PLANK:

1. Rinse the plank in water and allow it to dry.

2. Store the plank in a paper bag until the next use.

3. When you are ready to reuse the plank, resoak and preheat it. Preheating will only take a minute or two for a reused plank.

4. Do not reuse a plank that is completely charred and brittle. It is also not recommended to reuse planks after grilling fish, onions, or other strongly flavored foods. These flavors tend to stay in the wood and add unexpected flavors that may not complement the next recipe.

Plank Grilling Safety

As with any adventure, safety is a priority. The potential for fire exists when plank grilling. There are several guidelines to follow to avoid injury and to prevent fires. Even after the plank has been removed from the grill it is extremely hot and the potential for fire remains. Ensure that the plank has completely cooled before it is discarded. Always proceed with caution when handling, disposing of, or storing a used plank.

TO PLANK-GRILL SAFELY:

1. Always have water ready nearby. A spray bottle full of water or a garden hose are good precautionary items to have in case the plank ignites.

2. Always follow the manufacturer's safety guidelines for your grill.

3. Add a fire- or heat-proof oven mitt and a pair of tongs to your grilling accessories. Both are essential for handling a hot plank. Never handle a hot plank with bare hands.

4. Prepare a heat-proof area in which to place the plank once it has been removed from the grill.

5. Avoid getting the plank too close to the flame. The tip of the flame has extremely intense heat coming off it and will ignite your plank.

6. If you are unsure about your grill temperatures, err on the side of caution. Start grilling at a lower temperature setting and raise the heat until the desired amount of smoke is visible. The temperature varies inside all grills. As a result, smaller grills tend to take extra time to get hot, while larger grills tend to have higher intensity heat even at lower settings. Get acquainted with your grill's temperature at various settings prior to plank grilling.

7. Always plank-grill in a well-ventilated area, making sure that no smoke is drafting back into your house.

Plank Grilling Tips

It will not take long to feel comfortable with plank grilling because the learning curve increases at an exponential rate. You learn a lot with only your first few experiences. Remain patient with yourself or at least learn to laugh at yourself and have a plan B ready for your meal the first few times you practice with your plank. Following are a collection of tips that we wish we would have known up front when we started out. These general guidelines will put you a few steps ahead on your learning curve and will make it easier to truly master the art of plank grilling.

FOR GAS GRILLS:

1. Follow all Plank Preparation and Grilling guidelines on page xix prior to grilling.

2. Monitor the smoke during grilling. There will be a light smoke steadily flowing from your grill as the food cooks. The smoke should be light gray to white in color. You should always be able to see through the smoke. Smoke that is dark gray or black and difficult to see through is an indication that your plank has caught on fire.

3. It is not recommended to continually open the grill during the cooking process. However, if you desire a less intense smoky flavor, it can be achieved by raising the grill lid once or twice while cooking. We do caution that it is important to avoid opening the grill too often, as heat and flavor escape when the lid is removed.

4. To save time, you can presoak the planks and freeze them. Then just pull a plank out of the freezer and use it according to the same Plank Preparation and Grilling guidelines. Freezing the planks may, however, cause them to split due to the extreme heat change.

5. Once the planks become too charred and brittle, crumble them and spread them in the bottom of the grill to use as smoking chips.

6. While we have found that lamb and duck are some of the most delicious and succulent meats prepared on the plank, it is important to make enough just for the day it is being consumed. Unlike the other dishes prepared on the plank whose flavors are as good, if not better, on the following day, we think the lamb and duck dishes are best eaten the day they are prepared.

FOR CHARCOAL GRILLS:

1. Charcoal grills lose heat as the embers cool during grilling, which will increase the time needed for cooking. As all our recipes are based on gas grills, if you are grilling with charcoal, be prepared to add approximately 10 to 15 minutes to the cooking time called for in the recipes. For example, we found that a 1-inch halibut steak takes approximately 15 minutes to cook on a gas grill and 30 minutes to cook on a charcoal grill.

2. Smoke is key to perfectly plank-grilled food. Charcoal grills produce less smoke, but the smoky flavor is just as strong and delicious. It is very important to refrain from opening the lid during the grilling process.

3. The plank helps foods maintain their moisture by allowing them to cook in their own juices. The sauces and marinades used in our recipes also aid in moisture retention; however, try to avoid letting the sauces run over onto the briquettes as drippings will extinguish your flames.

Poultry

Gorgonzola *and* Spinach Chicken Rolls

Lemon Herb Roast Chicken

Chicken, Fig, *and* Pancetta Rolls *with*
  Balsamic Glaze

Orange *and* Bourbon Chicken Breasts

Chicken *with* Hot Pepper Jelly *and* Mustard Glaze

Chicken *with* Roasted Garlic Spread *and* Greens

Picnic Chicken Salad

Wild Rice, Pecan, Sausage, *and* Mushroom Stuffed
  Cornish Game Hens

Hot *and* Spicy Duck Breasts

Duck Egg Rolls

Duck *with* Wild Rice *and* Dried Cranberries

Orange Cinnamon Duck Breasts

Poultry is one of the most popular main entrées at today's dinner tables. However, it was not so long ago that poultry dishes were reserved for special occasions and holiday meals and game animals were the standard table fare. Today, there are many people who will not eat wild meat such as duck because of its "gamey" taste. If you are one of those people, try plank-grilling wild meat. We have discovered that grilling duck on a plank can mitigate those gamey flavors, infusing the meat with wood and smoke aromas and ultimately turning the overall experience into a culinary sensation not to be missed. A good example is *Duck Egg Rolls* (page 19), inspired by an Asian fusion–themed cooking club gathering. The plank is uniquely versatile because it eliminates tastes in meats that may be too strong and adds character and zest to meats that may otherwise be lacking them.

Poultry such as chicken and Cornish game hens also become food sensations on the grilling plank. One of the biggest challenges of cooking white meats is that they tend to dry out. Poultry dishes grilled on the plank come out incredibly juicy and moist. The plank even eliminates the brining process often performed prior to grilling poultry. As you will see with all of the recipes in this chapter, such as *Chicken, Fig, and Pancetta Rolls with Balsamic Glaze* (page 7), *Picnic Chicken Salad* (page 14), and *Orange and Bourbon Chicken Breasts* (page 9), the plank keeps the chicken tender and succulent.

Gorgonzola *and* Spinach Chicken Rolls

by: GRETCHEN BERNSDORFF

PLANK PREFERENCE: **CEDAR**

When I think about food, I think about what my body needs to be properly fueled. I try to consider low-fat options that are nutrient- and protein-dense. Chicken and spinach fit that description and are my usual go-to ingredients, but they tend to get boring. This recipe is my solution to bring some excitement to the palate. The bacon and cheese in this recipe, usually forbidden in my diet, make me think I am getting away with a treat. The truth is, many nutrients are fat-soluble, which means the body must have fat in order to absorb and utilize the nutrients in the spinach, red bell peppers, and chicken.

> 4 boneless, skinless chicken breasts
> Salt and pepper
> ½ teaspoon dried basil
> ½ teaspoon dried thyme
> 7 ounces crumbled Gorgonzola cheese
> One 7-ounce jar of roasted red bell peppers, thinly sliced
> 12 to 15 large spinach leaves
> 4 slices bacon, cooked and drained
> ¼ cup balsamic vinegar
> 2 to 3 tablespoons extra-virgin olive oil
> 4 toothpicks

Soak plank according to instructions on page xix.

Pound chicken by placing breast on solid surface and covering with a piece of plastic wrap or wax paper. Using the flat side of a mallet or the bottom of a frying pan, pound chicken to ¼-inch thickness. Repeat process for each breast.

Season both sides of chicken breasts with salt and pepper. Combine basil and thyme in a small bowl. Rub spice mixture into both sides of chicken breasts.

Lay out each chicken breast and layer with cheese, roasted red peppers, spinach, and bacon. Drizzle with vinegar. Starting at each edge, roll up chicken breast and pin with a toothpick.

Prepare plank for grilling according to instructions on page xx. Place chicken rolls on plank. Close lid and grill for 20 minutes, or until juices run clear. The rolls may need to be turned once to ensure they are cooked all the way through. Drizzle with olive oil just before serving.

MAKES 4 ROLLS

Lemon Herb Roast Chicken

by: MARIA EVERLY

PLANK PREFERENCE: **CEDAR**

My favorite place in my house is my dining room table. It is the one place where family and friends come together to share, rejoice, and fill the room with laughter. I enjoy hosting dinner parties and aim for recipes that are tasty, easy to prepare, serve many, and look beautiful on a plate. This dish offers all of that. The best part of it is that it can be made all year round. Grilling the chicken on a hot summer night brings the added benefit of not heating up the house. Once the chicken has cooled, I love to garnish it with fresh thyme and lemon slices around the platter. It is a beautiful centerpiece that will not disappoint. A nice white wine will suit the meal perfectly.

One 4½-pound whole chicken
4 tablespoons unsalted butter at room temperature
6 garlic cloves
5 fresh thyme sprigs
½ green onion, thinly sliced
Zest of 1 large lemon
1 leek, cleaned and cut lengthwise into 4 pieces, using about 1 to 2
　　inches of the green part
½ lemon cut into 3 slices
Salt and pepper

Soak plank according to instructions on page xix.

Rinse the chicken with cool water, inside and out. Pat dry with paper towels. Let chicken sit at room temperature while you make the butter spread.

To make the butter spread, combine 2 tablespoons butter, 2 thinly sliced garlic cloves, leaves from 2 of the thyme sprigs, green onion, and lemon zest. The spread will be chunky. Generously rub the spread under the skin of the chicken with clean hands.

Crush the remaining garlic cloves. Stuff the chicken cavity by layering in an alternating pattern the leeks, crushed garlic, lemon slices, remaining thyme sprigs, and 1 tablespoon unsalted butter that has been cut into thirds. Rub the outside of the chicken with remaining butter and season with salt and pepper.

Prepare plank for grilling according to instructions on page xx. Place chicken on plank. Close lid and grill for 50 to 55 minutes, or until a meat thermometer registers 170 degrees F in the breast meat and 185 degrees F in the thigh meat. When done, allow chicken to rest 10 minutes to allow the juices to settle and redistribute prior to carving. Place on serving platter and garnish with optional thyme and lemon slices.

Please note that this recipe can be quite messy on the grill and more than likely you will not be able to reuse the plank.

MAKES 4 SERVINGS

Chicken, Fig, *and* Pancetta Rolls *with* Balsamic Glaze

by: DINA GUILLEN

PLANK PREFERENCE: **CEDAR**

I am a kebab fanatic. If there is a cooking class on kebabs, I will take it. If there is a cookbook on kebabs, I will buy it. I love the concept of skewering all types of flavors together to form one mouthwatering dish. This elegant appetizer showcases the contrasting flavors presented when the spicy smokiness of cedar, the sweetness of figs, the mellowness of chicken, the savory saltiness of pancetta, and the tartness of balsamic vinegar meld together beautifully. Dried apricots can be substituted for the figs if you prefer.

   2 cups water
   10 dried figs, halved
   ½ cup plus 1 tablespoon balsamic vinegar
   ½ cup white wine
   2 tablespoons lemon juice
   2 tablespoons maple syrup
   1 tablespoon extra-virgin olive oil
   1 teaspoon chopped fresh thyme
   Salt and pepper
   2 boneless, skinless chicken breasts, cut into 1-inch cubes
      (about 20 pieces)
   20 pancetta slices, or 10 bacon slices, halved
   5 bamboo skewers, soaked in water for 1 hour

Soak plank according to instructions on page xix.

Bring water to a boil in a small saucepan. Reduce heat, add figs, and cook for 8 to 10 minutes until they have plumped up. Drain and set aside to cool.

To make the glaze, in a small saucepan mix ½ cup of the vinegar, white wine, lemon juice, and maple syrup. Bring to a boil over moderate heat until the mixture is reduced by half and becomes syrupy, about 10 minutes. Cover and keep warm.

In a large bowl, whisk remaining vinegar, oil, thyme, salt, and pepper. Add chicken and toss to coat. Place a fig half on each piece of chicken, wrap with 1 slice pancetta or bacon, and skewer to secure. Repeat until all pieces are skewered, leaving ¼ inch between each chicken roll.

Prepare plank for grilling according to instructions on page xx. Place chicken rolls on plank. Close lid and grill for 10 minutes.

To serve, allow chicken rolls to sit for 10 minutes before removing from skewers. Arrange on a serving platter and drizzle with balsamic vinegar glaze. Glaze can be served as a dip on the side if preferred.

MAKES 20 ROLLS

Orange *and* Bourbon Chicken Breasts

by: MICHELLE LOWREY

PLANK PREFERENCE: **ALL**

The flavor combination of orange and bourbon is a winner. Try not to pierce the chicken during cooking so the juices stay inside the meat. The whiskey can overpower the chicken, so do not marinate this longer than 8 hours.

- ½ **cup frozen orange juice, thawed**
- ¼ **cup bourbon whiskey**
- 2 **tablespoons lemon juice**
- 3 **large cloves garlic, crushed**
- 1 **teaspoon dried tarragon**
- ¼ **teaspoon salt**
- ¼ **teaspoon pepper**
- 4 **boneless, skinless chicken breasts**

Soak plank according to instructions on page xix.

To make the marinade, in a small bowl mix the orange juice, whiskey, lemon juice, garlic, and spices together. Put the chicken in a large glass baking dish. Add marinade, making sure the chicken is completely covered. Cover dish and marinate in refrigerator for at least 2 hours, but no longer than 8 hours.

Prepare plank for grilling according to instructions on page xx. Allow chicken to come to room temperature and place on plank. Grill for 25 minutes, or until juices run clear. Try to keep the grill closed as much as possible, but keep an eye out for flare-ups. Transfer chicken to a serving platter and cover with foil to rest for 5 minutes before serving.

MAKES 4 SERVINGS

Chicken *with* Hot Pepper Jelly *and* Mustard Glaze

by: MICHELLE LOWREY

PLANK PREFERENCE: **ALL**

When I was growing up, my mom was a big fan of canning and preserving fruits and vegetables of any kind. In late summer the big steamy mason jars would be lifted from the boiling water and filled with wonderful jellies, jams, and anything else she could think of. This process would go on for days and was a lot of hard work, but the pantry filled to the rafters with all the bounties of summer was a great source of pride to my mom. And every year, she would make her famous hot pepper jelly. She still makes it to this day, and last year her recipe won first place at the Lincoln County Fair in Oregon. Hot pepper jelly is a versatile sweet and spicy condiment. You can spoon it over a block of cream cheese for an instant appetizer or melt it down for use as a glaze. Although, in my opinion, there is nobody that makes a better hot pepper jelly than my mom, many wonderful brands are readily available at most grocery stores. With store-bought jelly, this recipe is a downright snap to make.

3 tablespoons unsalted butter
3 garlic cloves, crushed
¼ cup hot pepper jelly
2 tablespoons Dijon mustard
¼ teaspoon salt
¼ teaspoon pepper
4 chicken legs, skin on, with leg and thigh attached

Soak plank according to instructions on page xix.

In a small heavy-bottomed saucepan, melt butter and add garlic. Sauté for 1 minute over medium heat, being careful not to burn the garlic. Add the jelly, mustard, salt, and pepper and cook for an additional 5 minutes. Put the chicken in a large dish and pour glaze over chicken, coating well.

Prepare plank for grilling according to instructions on page xx. Place chicken on plank and grill for 25 to 30 minutes, or until juices run clear, keeping grill closed as much as possible. When chicken is done, turn off heat and allow chicken to sit inside grill for another 5 minutes before transferring it to a serving platter. If using a charcoal barbecue, remove chicken from grill immediately and hold in warm area for 5 minutes before serving.

MAKES 4 SERVINGS

Chicken *with* **Roasted Garlic Spread** *and* **Greens**

by: **MARIA EVERLY**

PLANK PREFERENCE: **ALDER**

I *live a stone's throw away from Napa Valley, California—our nation's wine country. I take full advantage of this and make frequent visits to experience the ambiance, the wines, and most of all the culinary delights. During one visit over lunch with friends, I had a grilled chicken salad that made my mouth water and my mind work. The salad left an imprint, a lingering impression. Needless to say, I was inspired. The result was this very colorful bistro salad. The roasted garlic and fresh herbs give the chicken that perfect touch; the simple vinegar and olive oil dressing wonderfully blends contrasting flavors; and the wood gives the chicken a subtle, smoky taste and enables it to stay moist.*

1 whole head garlic
6 tablespoons extra-virgin olive oil, plus more to coat garlic
Salt
1 stick unsalted butter at room temperature
8 fresh thyme sprigs, leaves plucked and minced
2 teaspoons fresh lemon juice
4 boneless, skinless chicken breasts
2 tablespoons red wine vinegar
Pepper
6 to 8 cups spring salad mix or mizuna greens
1 small cucumber, thinly sliced with skin left on
1 medium red bell pepper, thinly sliced
1 medium yellow bell pepper, thinly sliced
Crumbled Gorgonzola or feta cheese

Soak plank according to instructions on page xix.

To make the roasted garlic spread, preheat oven to 350 degrees F. Cut the top quarter from the head of garlic and discard; drizzle the remainder with olive oil and sprinkle with salt. Put in oven-safe bowl or on aluminum foil and bake for

30 to 45 minutes, or until garlic turns creamy and tender. Remove from oven and allow to cool for 30 minutes.

Once garlic has cooled, squeeze cloves into an electric mixer bowl. Add butter, thyme, and 1 teaspoon lemon juice and mix on medium-high for about 1 minute, or until consistency of spread is smooth. If a mixer is not available, you can combine mixture by hand with a spoon. Season with salt to taste and set aside.

Spread roasted garlic spread on both sides of chicken breasts until well coated. Set aside.

Prepare plank for grilling according to instructions on page xx. Place chicken on plank. Close lid and grill for about 30 minutes, or until juices run clear. Remove chicken from grill and allow to sit for 5 minutes.

To make the salad, while chicken is resting whisk vinegar, the remaining lemon juice, and 6 tablespoons olive oil. Season with salt and pepper to taste. Toss the salad greens, cucumber, and red and yellow bell peppers with enough dressing to moisten. Place greens on individual plates.

Slice each chicken breast diagonally and place over greens. Sprinkle with Gorgonzola. Serve immediately and enjoy!

MAKES 4 SERVINGS

Picnic Chicken Salad

by: **MARIA EVERLY**

PLANK PREFERENCE: **CEDAR** *or* **ALDER**

I am a sucker for romance. The sappier the story, the further I fall in love. Whether on an ocean bluff, creekside, or in a country field filled with wildflowers, to me there is nothing more romantic than a picnic. Chicken salad is delicious anytime and this recipe is ideal for a spring or summer picnic. It is easy to prepare and particularly great if it is made a day ahead. In your picnic basket bring along an assortment of fruits and cheeses, a mixed green salad, lemon pound cake, and a bottle of blush wine. Spoon the chicken salad over bruschetta, focaccia, or a rustic bread, and enjoy laughing and sharing the day with a love or family and friends. But remember, the most important ingredient here is love, so bring lots of it along—you are bound to have a delightful time.

> **2 boneless, skinless chicken breasts**
> **Macadamia nut oil or extra-virgin olive oil to coat**
> **Salt and pepper**
> **2 celery stalks, finely diced**
> **3 green onions, finely chopped, both green and white parts**
> **½ cup finely diced red onion**
> **½ red apple, finely diced**
> **1 tablespoon chopped fresh basil or parsley**
> **½ cup mayonnaise**
> **2 tablespoons fresh lemon juice**

Soak plank according to instructions on page xix.

Coat chicken with oil. Season with salt and pepper to taste. Set chicken aside and allow it to come to room temperature, about 30 minutes.

Prepare plank for grilling according to instructions on page xx. Place chicken on plank. Close lid and grill for 30 minutes, or until juices run clear. Remove chicken from grill and allow to cool for about 20 minutes.

Slice each chicken breast into 4 to 6 pieces. This will make it easier to pull apart. Using your hands, over a medium bowl, pull apart chicken into bite-size pieces.

Combine celery, green onions, red onion, apple, and basil in a medium bowl. Add shredded chicken, mayonnaise, and lemon juice. Season with salt and pepper to taste. Gently mix until all ingredients are combined.

Place in refrigerator to cool for several hours, or make a day ahead. When ready to serve, remove from refrigerator and gently mix. Spoon chicken salad over bruschetta or serve on your favorite bread.

MAKES 4 SERVINGS

Wild Rice, Pecan, Sausage, *and* Mushroom Stuffed Cornish Game Hens

by: **MARIA EVERLY**

PLANK PREFERENCE: **ALL**

Autumn is one of my favorite seasons, and I particularly love the burnished tones that the season showcases. I enjoy the drop in temperature, sitting by a roaring fire, millions of fallen leaves on the ground, and the abundant harvest of apples, pumpkins, and pears. Not only does it signify the soon-to-be holiday season, but it is also a time to enjoy hardier, warm meals. To me, Cornish game hens are the perfect autumn meal. The golden hens are moist, smoky, and succulent and laced with nutty, toasted flavors. The stuffing below is great in Thanksgiving turkey as well.

  4 Cornish game hens
  Extra-virgin olive oil to coat
  Salt and pepper
  ¼ teaspoon dried thyme
  ⅓ pound pork sausage
  ¼ cup finely diced onion
  ½ medium zucchini, finely diced
  2 cremini mushrooms, cleaned and finely diced
  1 cup cooked long-grain wild rice mix
  ¼ cup pecans, finely chopped

Soak plank according to instructions on page xix.

Clean cavity of hens; rinse and pat dry with paper towels. Brush with olive oil and season with salt, pepper, and thyme. Set aside.

To make the stuffing, in a small nonstick pan, brown sausage for 8 to 10 minutes, separating it into small bits. Drain all but 1 teaspoon of oil from pan. Add onion, zucchini, and mushrooms and sauté until soft, about 5 minutes.

Add sausage mixture to the rice. Add pecans and mix well. Season with salt and pepper to taste.

Stuff game hens with sausage-and-rice mixture. Truss legs with cooking string that has been soaked in water to avoid burning on grill.

Prepare plank for grilling according to instructions on page xx. Place stuffed game hens on plank. Close lid and grill for about 40 minutes, or until cavity reaches 165 degrees F. Remove hens from plank and allow to sit for 5 minutes before serving.

MAKES 4 SERVINGS

Hot *and* Spicy Duck Breasts

by: GRETCHEN BERNSDORFF

PLANK PREFERENCE: **ALDER**

Living in California has allowed me to expand beyond my comfort zone and add a variety of ethnic foods to my menus, especially Mexican dishes. The typical Mexican spices in this recipe pack heat and give the duck a bold essence without over-powering it. The sour cream gives a cooling impression and then the Tabasco surprises you with a little extra taste sensation. Serve this dish over grits. Having been born and raised in the South, I not only know what grits are but I know what to do with them. So trust me, duck prepared this way goes excellently with grits instead of tortillas or rice.

½ teaspoon ground black pepper
1 teaspoon chili powder
½ teaspoon ground cumin
1 teaspoon celery salt
Two ½-pound duck breasts, skin on
Tabasco sauce
3 tablespoons sour cream

Soak plank according to instructions on page xix.

In a small bowl, combine the pepper, chili powder, cumin, and celery salt. Peel the skin back on the duck breast, but leave it attached along one edge. Rub the pepper mixture on all surfaces of the duck, including under the skin and on the skin itself. Replace skin when finished.

Prepare plank for grilling according to instructions on page xx. Place duck on the plank. Close lid and grill for 25 minutes. Duck should be slightly pink in the center when done. Remove meat from plank. Remove skin from breast meat and slice.

Combine a few dashes of Tabasco with the sour cream in a small serving bowl. Serve the sliced duck with a dollop of the sour cream mixture. If desired, a few dashes of Tabasco can also be added to the duck itself. Watch out for the kick!

MAKES 2 SERVINGS

Duck Egg Rolls

by: GRETCHEN BERNSDORFF

PLANK PREFERENCE: **CEDAR**

*A*s a child I was the definition of a picky eater. Despite the incredible cooks my mom, grandmothers, and sister were, I was so picky that cereal, grilled cheese sandwiches, and SpaghettiOs were the only reason I made it to adulthood. I managed to find a way to feed everything else to the cats. For ages I could not imagine eating dark meat, much less duck. But since I began plank grilling, I crave plank-grilled duck. The plank completely infuses the duck, imparting flavors of incredible depth. These egg rolls are packed full of taste sensations that are out of this world.

2 tablespoons ketchup
1 tablespoon hoisin sauce
¼ cup reduced-sodium soy sauce
1 tablespoon clam juice
¼ teaspoon dried ground ginger
2 tablespoons pineapple juice
Two ½-pound duck breasts, thinly sliced, skins reserved
3 tablespoons sesame oil
2 celery stalks, thinly sliced (nearly shredded)
3 green onions, thinly sliced (nearly shredded)
6 ounces fresh oyster or porcini mushrooms, diced
1 cup shredded green cabbage and carrots
10 egg roll wrappers
Canola oil
Hot mustard, sweet and sour, or any other dipping sauce

Soak plank according to instructions on page xix.

In a medium bowl, whisk together ketchup, hoisin sauce, soy sauce, clam juice, ginger, and pineapple juice. Add sliced duck and reserved skins, making sure marinade covers meat. Cover, refrigerate, and marinate overnight.

Drain marinade from duck and let duck come to room temperature, about 30 minutes.

Prepare plank for grilling according to instructions on page xx. Place duck on plank and cover with skin. Close lid and grill for 15 minutes, or until duck is no longer pink. Remove the duck from plank, discard skins, and allow to cool slightly. Dice breast meat and set aside.

Heat sesame oil in large skillet over medium-high heat. Add celery, green onions, and mushrooms and sauté until tender. Add cabbage and carrot mixture. Stir until warmed and well coated. Remove from heat and allow to cool slightly.

Combine diced duck and vegetable mixture. Place about 2 tablespoons of duck mixture in an egg roll wrapper and fold according to the package instructions. Use a drop of water to seal the egg roll closed.

Heat canola oil in a deep frying pan to 350 degrees F. Drop egg rolls into oil and fry until golden brown. Remove to paper towel to drain. Serve hot with dipping sauce.

MAKES 10 EGG ROLLS

Duck *with* **Wild Rice** *and* **Dried Cranberries**

by: GRETCHEN BERNSDORFF

PLANK PREFERENCE: **CEDAR**

O*ne way to create a recipe is to think about the flavors in a favorite wine. I knew duck paired well with syrah and petite sirah wines, so in thinking about the rich, complex tastes of these wines I selected ingredients to match. The tastes of these wines include wild berries, pepper, licorice, cocoa, and earth. That same flavor structure is complemented by the cranberries, curry, mustard, and mushrooms of this recipe.*

Two ½-pound duck breasts, skin on
¼ teaspoon curry powder
2 tablespoons sesame oil
½ teaspoon coarse-ground mustard
1 package wild rice mix
One 14-ounce can chicken broth
6 slices bacon
One 8-ounce package sliced mushrooms
¾ cup dried cranberries
Salt and pepper

Soak plank according to instructions on page xix.

Separate skin from duck meat, but leave attached along one edge. In a small bowl, whisk together curry, oil, and mustard. Thoroughly coat all surfaces of duck with oil mixture. Cover, refrigerate, and marinate overnight.

Prepare plank for grilling according to instructions on page xx. Place duck on plank. Close lid and grill for 25 minutes. Duck should be slightly pink in the center when done. Discard skin and cut duck into bite-size pieces. Set aside.

While duck is grilling, cook rice according to package instructions using chicken broth instead of water.

In a large skillet, fry bacon until crisp. Drain on a paper towel. Drain all but 3 tablespoons bacon fat from skillet. Over medium heat, sauté mushrooms until tender. Add duck and ½ cup of cranberries to mushrooms. Toss to coat and remove from heat.

Crumble bacon and place in a large serving bowl. Add duck mixture and 1 cup cooked rice (reserve remaining rice for another use) to bacon and combine. Season with salt and pepper to taste. Top with remaining cranberries and serve.

MAKES 4 TO 6 SERVINGS

Orange Cinnamon Duck Breasts

by: GRETCHEN BERNSDORFF

PLANK PREFERENCE: **ALDER**

Ifind stargazing particularly comforting because it reminds me of my father. On clear, warm summer nights we would climb to the rooftop on a ladder and lay side by side on the warm shingles, our eyes fixed on the heavens. He would point out stars and planets by name, and I would try my best to remember them. I don't remember being more at peace than on those nights. Standing out at the grill after several failed attempts at new recipes, I was frazzled and frantic to find inspiration. Naturally, I looked to the stars and was immediately calmed. The pressure gone, in no time I had this recipe to add to my comfort-food repertoire. The sweetness of the marmalade and preserves combined with the butter and maple give the duck an essence that is rich and seductive. The orange-flavored rum adds a surprisingly sublime citrus note. The final dimension for balancing the succulence of the duck is the familiarity of cinnamon and nutmeg. Wild duck is very lean so it is important to plank-grill it with the skin intact. The plank will capture the juices and keep the meat moist.

½ teaspoon cinnamon plus more for the sauce
½ teaspoon dried ground ginger
½ teaspoon nutmeg
1 tablespoon orange marmalade
Two ½-pound duck breasts, skin on
¼ cup Bacardi O rum, or ¼ cup white rum with 1 tablespoon
    orange juice
2 tablespoons extra-virgin olive oil
1 tablespoon apricot preserves
1 tablespoon honey
¼ teaspoon maple extract
1 tablespoon butter
½ teaspoon sugar

Soak plank according to instructions on page xix.

In a small bowl, combine ½ teaspoon cinnamon, ginger, nutmeg, and marmalade. Peel the skin back on the breast meat, but leave it attached along one edge. Completely coat all the surfaces of the duck with the cinnamon mixture, replacing the skin when done.

Prepare plank for grilling according to instructions on page xx. Place duck on the plank. Close lid and grill for 25 minutes. Duck should be slightly pink in the center when done. Remove and discard skin.

To make the sauce, combine the rum, olive oil, preserves, honey, maple extract, butter, and sugar in a small saucepan over medium heat. Bring to a boil, reduce heat, and simmer 5 to 8 minutes. Add a dash or two of cinnamon. Stir well to completely fold in the cinnamon and remove from heat.

Slice duck and serve with sauce.

MAKES 2 SERVINGS

Beef, Lamb, *and* Pork

Meat Loaf *with* Tomato *and* Red Pepper Sauce

Beef Tri-Tip Roast *with a* Cherry Tomato Festival

Amaretto Flank Steak

Filet Mignon *in* Port Wine Mushroom Sauce

Beef Tenderloin Steaks Topped *with* Butter Spread

Bacon Portobello Mushroom Burgers

Pork Tenderloin *with* Blackberry Mustard Sauce

Pork Baby Back Ribs *with* Sweet Barbecue Sauce

Pistachio Lemon Stuffed Pork Chops

Apple Pecan Stuffed Pork Chops

Pork Chops *with* Honey Balsamic Glaze

Orange *and* Sesame Pork Tenderloin

Juniper *and* Porcini Lamb Chops

Curry *and* Ginger Lamb Chops *with* Spicy Peach Sauce

Sizzling Lamb Fajitas

Rack *of* Lamb *over* Rosemary Pomegranate Sauce

Lamb *and* Potato Kebabs

Remember back to the last grand meal you enjoyed and chances are it included beef or another substantial cut of meat. Whether it was the prime rib at your best friend's wedding, the rack of lamb over Christmas dinner, or a pork tenderloin at your favorite hideaway, hearty meats are always a crowd pleaser.

Grilling beef, lamb, or pork on a plank will ensure a meal to remember. Each cut of meat will be flavorful, moist, and smoky due to the indirect-heat cooking method, which allows the meat to cook evenly while retaining its moisture. Dishes with sauces or marinades like *Beef Tenderloin Steaks Topped with Butter Spread* (page 35), *Filet Mignon in Port Wine Mushroom Sauce* (page 33), and *Pork Tenderloin with Blackberry Mustard Sauce* (page 38) produce stunning results. Because wood planks tend to bow slightly upward due to the intense heat, sauces and marinades stay with the meat during the grilling process more than they would without the plank. The result is moist meat packed with the flavor of the sauce and the wonderful smoky taste that only a plank can deliver.

Because the food is insulated from direct heat, entrées such as *Meat Loaf with Tomato and Red Pepper Sauce* (page 27) will not burn and will be healthier table fare because some of the fat drains off and burns away during the grilling process. The exterior of the meat loaf will be browned while the plank keeps the inside moist. Lamb aficionados will be very pleased with how a plank brings out the flavor of the lamb and fears of a gamey taste are squashed thanks to the smoky goodness a plank delivers. Great cooking always involves great ingredients and a plank is just that—a great ingredient. So cinch up that apron, gather family and friends, and start creating new memories.

Meat Loaf *with* Tomato *and* Red Pepper Sauce

by: DINA GUILLEN

PLANK PREFERENCE: **ALL**

I never understood the big deal about meat loaf. It is my husband's favorite meal on earth, and I would reluctantly make it once a year on his birthday. Then I tried plank-grilling meat loaf and I am hooked. I love this recipe—the smoke and wood's flavor permeates the meat loaf, bacon, and sauce as it grills. This recipe takes a while to prepare since there are a lot of vegetables that need fine chopping and sautéing, and grilling takes another hour and 10 minutes, but the time required is very much worthwhile. You can save some time, however, by making the sauce up to three days in advance.

2 tablespoons extra-virgin olive oil
1½ cups finely chopped onion
½ red bell pepper, finely chopped
1 stalk celery, finely chopped
6 garlic cloves, minced
½ cup cremini mushrooms, finely chopped
1 teaspoon chopped fresh thyme, or ¼ teaspoon dried
1 teaspoon chopped fresh rosemary, or ¼ teaspoon dried
2 large eggs
½ cup milk
2 teaspoons Dijon mustard
1 tablespoon Worcestershire sauce
⅓ cup ketchup
1 teaspoon salt
¼ teaspoon black pepper
1 pound ground beef
½ pound ground veal
½ pound pork sausage
1 cup bread crumbs
5 slices bacon, halved
3 cups Tomato and Red Pepper Sauce (recipe follows)

Soak plank according to instructions on page xix.

Heat olive oil over moderate heat in a large nonstick skillet. Add onion, bell pepper, and celery and cook, stirring occasionally, until vegetables are softened and beginning to brown around the edges, about 5 minutes. Add the garlic, mushrooms, thyme, and rosemary. Cook until the liquid the mushrooms give off is evaporated and they are very tender, 10 to 15 minutes. Cooking the vegetables first allows the water from vegetables to escape and avoids breaking up the meat loaf. Remove skillet from heat, set aside, and allow to cool completely.

In a large mixing bowl, whisk together the eggs, milk, mustard, Worcestershire sauce, ketchup, salt, and pepper. Stir in the cooled vegetable mixture. (Make sure the vegetables are completely cool before adding to meat, otherwise they will cook the meat and eggs.) Stir in the meats and bread crumbs and mix until just combined. Do not overmix or the meat will get tough. To test for seasoning, take a teaspoon of meat loaf mixture and cook in skillet. Adjust seasoning if needed.

Prepare plank for grilling according to instructions on page xx. Spoon the meat loaf mixture onto the plank and form into a loaf. Arrange the slices of bacon on top, then carefully spoon sauce over uncooked loaf. Grill for 1 hour and 10 minutes, or until juices run clear. Remove plank from grill and let sit for 10 minutes before serving.

MAKES 8 SERVINGS

TOMATO *and* RED PEPPER SAUCE

½ cup ketchup
2 plum tomatoes, diced
½ red bell pepper, chopped
½ cup chopped onion
1 teaspoon dry mustard
2 tablespoons red wine vinegar
2 tablespoons Worcestershire sauce
2 large garlic cloves, minced
1 teaspoon chopped fresh flat-leaf parsley
½ teaspoon salt
¼ teaspoon black pepper

In a medium saucepan, combine all ingredients over medium-high heat and bring to a boil. Lower heat and simmer for 7 minutes until sauce slightly thickens.

MAKES 3 CUPS

Beef Tri-Tip Roast *with a* Cherry Tomato Festival

by: MARIA EVERLY

PLANK PREFERENCE: **ALDER** *or* **MAPLE**

*O*ne of my favorite things about summer is visiting the local farmer's market. I love the smells and the feel of the ripe fruits and vegetables. In my eyes, nothing compares to cooking with local seasonal foods. This recipe is filled with seasonal festive flavors. On a hot summer day what can be more satisfying than a juicy cut of meat hot off the grill topped with fresh herbs and vine-ripe tomatoes? Pair this dish with a field greens salad, garlic herb roasted potatoes, green beans, or fresh corn on the cob.

½ cup Worcestershire sauce
½ cup extra-virgin olive oil
4 garlic cloves, crushed
2 tablespoons finely chopped shallots
3 to 4 fresh rosemary sprigs
½ teaspoon salt plus more to taste
¼ teaspoon pepper plus more to taste
One 2-pound tri-tip roast
1 cup red cherry tomatoes, halved
1 cup yellow cherry tomatoes, halved
2 green onions, finely chopped
6 fresh basil leaves
6 fresh oregano sprigs, leaves plucked and stems discarded
3 tablespoons balsamic vinegar

Soak plank according to instructions on page xix.

To make the marinade, in a small mixing bowl combine Worcestershire, ¼ cup olive oil, garlic, shallots, rosemary, ½ teaspoon salt, and ¼ teaspoon pepper and mix well. Pour marinade over tri-tip roast in shallow dish or large resealable plastic bag. Refrigerate overnight or for a minimum of 4 hours and up to 24 hours.

Remove meat from refrigerator and allow to warm to room temperature, about 30 minutes. Prepare plank for grilling according to instructions on page xx.

In a medium bowl, combine red and yellow cherry tomatoes, green onions, basil, and oregano. Set aside.

Place meat on plank. Close lid and grill for about 30 to 35 minutes for medium. Remove from grill and allow meat to rest for about 8 to 10 minutes. While meat is resting, pour the remaining olive oil and balsamic vinegar over prepared tomato mixture. Season with salt and pepper to taste and mix gently.

Slice meat against the grain, and serve topped with cherry tomato mixture.

MAKES 4 TO 6 SERVINGS

Amaretto Flank Steak

by: **GRETCHEN BERNSDORFF**

PLANK PREFERENCE: **ALDER**

Pair this steak with your favorite plank-grilled vegetable and a steaming-hot baked potato and you have created a meal right off the pages of a restaurant menu. I like to put the flank steak in the marinade and into the refrigerator before going to bed. In the morning, I flip it over before going to work, and it is all ready to go when I get home.

> 2 tablespoons sesame oil
> ¼ cup soy sauce
> 2 tablespoons molasses
> 6 tablespoons amaretto liqueur
> ¼ cup brown sugar
> 2 teaspoons dried ground ginger
> 2 tablespoons white wine Worcestershire sauce
> 3 garlic cloves, minced
> 1½ pounds flank steak

Soak plank according to instructions on page xix.

To make the marinade, combine all ingredients except the flank steak in a 1-gallon resealable plastic bag. Add the flank steak and completely coat the meat with the marinade. Place the bag on a plate to catch any possible drips and refrigerate all day or overnight.

Prepare plank for grilling according to instructions on page xx. Place flank steak on plank. Close lid and grill for about 15 minutes for medium-rare. Pull the meat off just before you think it is done. The meat will finish cooking on its own while resting.

Slice the meat on a cutting board that will allow you to recapture the juices. Place the meat on a serving platter and pour the reclaimed juices over the top.

MAKES 4 SERVINGS

Filet Mignon *in* Port Wine Mushroom Sauce

by: MICHELLE LOWREY

PLANK PREFERENCE: **CEDAR**

When you want to bring out the big guns, nothing impresses better than a beautiful filet mignon. Back when I was dating my now-husband Corey, this was the first dish I made for him to show off my talents in the kitchen. We met in college, so buying filet mignon was very extravagant and way out of our everyday budget. We have been happily married for more than twelve years now, and to this day, filet mignon is the dish I prepare for our special occasions. The sweetness of the cedar plank complements the port sauce nicely. Serve this with a simple salad for a truly special meal.

4 slices pepper bacon
Four 1¼- to 1½-inch filets mignons, 2 to 3 pounds total
1 tablespoon salt
1 tablespoon freshly cracked black pepper
4 large garlic cloves, minced
Port Wine Mushroom Sauce (recipe follows)
Toothpicks for securing meat

Soak plank according to instructions on page xix.

Wrap a slice of bacon around each filet, securing with toothpicks. Sprinkle both sides of meat with salt and pepper. Spread garlic liberally over both sides of steak and set aside.

Prepare plank for grilling according to instructions on page xx. Place steaks on plank. Close lid and grill for 10 minutes. Turn steaks over. Close lid and grill until desired doneness, about 3 to 4 minutes for medium-rare. Place steaks on platter, cover with foil, and allow to rest for 5 minutes.

While steaks are resting, reheat port sauce. Spoon over filets and serve.

MAKES 4 SERVINGS

PORT WINE MUSHROOM SAUCE

2 tablespoons unsalted butter
½ cup mushrooms, coarsely chopped
2 teaspoons minced fresh rosemary, or 1 teaspoon dried
¼ cup port
½ cup beef stock
¼ cup heavy cream

Heat butter in a medium skillet over medium heat until it starts to foam. Turn heat up to medium-high and add mushrooms and rosemary. Cook until mushrooms are golden and slightly caramelized, about 5 minutes. Add port and beef stock and simmer until mixture starts to reduce, about 8 minutes. Add heavy cream to skillet and boil until mixture is thickened, stirring constantly.

MAKES ABOUT 2 CUPS

Beef Tenderloin Steaks Topped *with* Butter Spread

by: **MARIA EVERLY**

PLANK PREFERENCE: **MAPLE**

These steaks are ideal for either a casual summer barbecue or a black-tie affair. The maple smoke brings out the rich flavor of beef tenderloin in this special recipe that will leave your guests asking for more. Finish the tenderloins with the simple yet mouthwatering butter spread, and pair with roasted potatoes and a fine full-bodied red wine. A perfect meal for the perfect night.

¼ cup butter at room temperature
1 tablespoon Worcestershire sauce
1¾ teaspoons ground black pepper
¼ teaspoon salt
¼ cup stone-ground mustard, or any seed-style Dijon mustard
¼ cup soy sauce
2 tablespoons garlic powder
¼ cup brown sugar
2 tablespoons chopped shallots
2 garlic cloves, coarsely chopped (not pressed)
¼ cup chopped roasted red bell pepper
½ cup extra-virgin olive oil
Four 6- to 8-ounce beef tenderloin steaks
Cremini or shiitake mushrooms (optional)

Soak plank according to instructions on page xix.

To make the butter spread, in a small bowl combine butter, Worcestershire sauce, ¼ teaspoon pepper, and salt. Mix with an electric mixer or by hand until fully combined. Spread butter mixture on wax paper sheet and roll into a log. Butter sauce can be made up to three days ahead.

To make the marinade, in a small bowl combine remaining pepper, mustard, soy sauce, garlic powder, brown sugar, shallots, garlic, and roasted red pepper. Pour all ingredients into a food processor or blender and mix slowly. Add oil until the mixture thickens into a mayonnaise-like consistency. Spread marinade on steaks and place in a large shallow pan or large resealable plastic bag. Refrigerate for a minimum of 4 hours and up to 24 hours. The longer you marinate the steaks, the more intense the flavor.

Remove steaks from refrigerator 30 minutes before grilling to bring to room temperature. Remove butter spread from refrigerator. Cut four ½-inch pieces and set aside.

Prepare plank for grilling according to instructions on page xx. Remove excess marinade from steaks and place steaks on plank. Top steaks with mushrooms, if using. Close lid and grill 10 to 15 minutes for medium-rare. Remove steaks from grill and top with butter spread. Allow steaks to rest for 5 minutes and serve.

MAKES 4 SERVINGS

Bacon Portobello Mushroom Burgers

by: **MARIA EVERLY**

PLANK PREFERENCE: **ALL**

I grew up as a tomboy, a free spirit who lived on fruits and vegetables. As a youth I considered myself a vegetarian. In fact, I think I had my first hamburger at age eighteen while on a date. I guess you can say that I fell in love. I married that man who introduced me to hamburgers, and now I find ways of adding a twist to the traditional American burger. A plank infuses subtle flavor as it allows the meat to maintain its moisture, making one of the juiciest hamburgers you will ever eat. Easy to prepare and well-suited to any occasion, this recipe can easily be multiplied depending on the size of your party. Pair this with fresh corn on the cob, baked beans, or pasta—and enjoy.

> 1 pound lean ground beef
> 1 small portobello mushroom, cleaned and finely diced
> 1 small shallot, finely diced
> ¼ cup real bacon bits
> 1 egg, beaten
> 2 tablespoons barbecue sauce
> ½ teaspoon seasoning salt
> 1 tablespoon butter, cut into four pieces
> 4 slices smoked Gouda cheese
> 4 hamburger buns
> Lettuce, tomato, and any desired condiments (optional)

Soak plank according to instructions on page xix.

In large bowl combine ground beef, mushroom, shallot, bacon bits, egg, barbecue sauce, and seasoning salt. With your hands, mix until combined, and form into four hamburger patties. In the center of each patty, insert a butter square and re-form the patty to cover. Refrigerate for 30 minutes.

Prepare plank for grilling according to instructions on page xx. Place hamburger patties on plank. Close lid and grill for about 8 to 10 minutes for medium-rare, or until desired doneness. Remove from grill and place one slice of cheese on each burger and allow to rest for 5 minutes. Serve on hamburger buns along with desired vegetables and condiments.

MAKES 4 HAMBURGERS

Pork Tenderloin *with* Blackberry Mustard Sauce

by: MICHELLE LOWREY

PLANK PREFERENCE: **ALL**

The tenderloin in this recipe is brined, a favorite way of mine to prepare pork for the grill. I love how juicy and succulent the meat is when cooked this way. The Blackberry Mustard Sauce is delicious and can be served over chicken and fish too. Place the tenderloin in the brine mixture before leaving for work to be ready to grill when you get home. Don't be alarmed by the slight pink color of the meat; that's just the brine mixture doing its magic!

8 cups water
½ cup sugar
½ cup kosher salt
4 teaspoons pure vanilla extract
1 tablespoon freshly cracked black pepper
1 tablespoon ground allspice
1 teaspoon whole cloves
2 pork tenderloins, 1 to 1¼ pounds each, silvery skin and fat removed
2 tablespoons extra-virgin olive oil
1½ cups Blackberry Mustard Sauce (recipe follows)

Soak plank according to instructions on page xix.

To make brine mixture, boil 2 cups water in a large saucepan over medium-high heat and add sugar and salt. Stir until completely dissolved. Add remaining cold water, vanilla, and spices, stirring to combine.

Place brine mixture in a large bowl and add tenderloins, making sure that the pork is completely submerged in brine. A heavy plate works well for this. Keep tenderloins in the brine for 6 to 8 hours, covered in the refrigerator. You can keep the pork in the brine for up to 14 hours. Any longer and the texture of the meat can become rubbery. After brining pork, rinse completely in cold water twice, making sure all spices are removed. Discard brining liquid and store tenderloins until ready to use.

Prepare plank for grilling according to instructions on page xx. Coat tenderloins with olive oil and place them on plank. Close lid and grill for 15 minutes. Turn off grill and continue to cook meat with the grill lid closed for an additional 5 to 7 minutes. Using a meat thermometer, grill meat until cooked to an internal temperature between 145 and 150 degrees F for medium doneness.

Remove meat from grill and transfer to cutting board. Cover loosely with foil and allow meat to rest for an additional 5 minutes. The meat will continue to cook while resting. To serve, cut tenderloin into ½-inch slices and serve with warmed Blackberry Mustard Sauce.

MAKES 6 SERVINGS

BLACKBERRY MUSTARD SAUCE

3 tablespoons unsalted butter
2 small garlic cloves, chopped
1 cup red wine
2 tablespoons coarse-ground mustard
2 tablespoons balsamic vinegar
¼ teaspoon ground cumin
1 cup seedless blackberry jam

In a heavy-bottomed medium saucepan, melt 2 tablespoons butter over medium-high heat. Add garlic and cook until the garlic just begins to brown. Add wine, mustard, vinegar, and cumin and bring to a boil. Turn heat to medium and simmer until slightly reduced, about 10 to 12 minutes. Remove from heat and set aside.

Just before serving, reheat mustard sauce over medium heat, adding blackberry jam and remaining butter.

MAKES 1½ CUPS

Pork Baby Back Ribs *with* Sweet Barbecue Sauce

by: **MARIA EVERLY**

PLANK PREFERENCE: **ALL**

One spring afternoon in Austin, Texas, my husband, Farres, and I were lucky enough to stumble on a barnyard barbecue. The food was great, the beer was cold, and Reckless Kelly never sounded better. That afternoon, I became a fan of barbecue ribs and barbecue sauce. Years later, I tried my hand at creating my own barbecue sauce. Through trial and error and many modifications I landed on a recipe that is simple, slightly sweet, and can be used on countless dishes. The ribs are a satisfying meal best eaten with your hands and they are worth the effort and messy drips. To save time, the barbecue sauce can be made a day ahead.

    3 tablespoons extra-virgin olive oil
    1 medium onion, chopped
    2 tablespoons finely chopped shallots
    2 garlic cloves, finely chopped
    1 cup tomato sauce, or ketchup
    ⅓ cup full-flavored molasses
    ¼ cup dark brown sugar
    ¼ cup orange juice
    1 tablespoon Worcestershire sauce
    ½ teaspoon salt plus more to taste
    ¼ teaspoon freshly ground black pepper plus more to taste
    2 pounds baby back ribs

Soak plank according to instructions on page xix.

To make the sauce, in a medium saucepan heat the oil over medium-high heat. Reduce heat to medium and add the onion, shallots, and garlic. Gently sauté for about 10 minutes. Add the tomato sauce, molasses, brown sugar, orange juice, Worcestershire sauce, ½ teaspoon salt, and ¼ teaspoon pepper. Mix well and bring to a boil. Reduce heat and simmer for about 30 minutes, stirring occasionally, until sauce is slightly thickened and reduced by half.

Remove sauce from stove and pour through a fine sieve into a medium bowl. Press the solids against the sieve with a spoon until all the sauce is drained into the bowl. Discard solids and set sauce aside.

Prepare plank for grilling according to instructions on page xx. Season ribs with salt and pepper. Place rib rack on plank facedown. Close lid and grill for 15 minutes. Turn ribs over, close lid, and cook an additional 15 minutes. During the last 7 minutes brush the barbecue sauce on the ribs. Do not brush the sauce on earlier because the sugar in the sauce will burn. Remove ribs from grill and allow to cool for about 5 minutes. Cut ribs between bones and serve.

MAKES 2 SERVINGS

Pistachio Lemon Stuffed Pork Chops

by: **DINA GUILLEN**

PLANK PREFERENCE: **ALL**

Before I discovered plank grilling, I rarely grilled pork chops without brining them first, since they would inevitably come out dry. Plank grilling is perfect for cuts of meat like pork chops since the smoke helps the meat retain moisture. This recipe includes a wonderfully delicious stuffing that adds even more moisture, making this dish very juicy and tender.

> 1 cup fresh bread crumbs
> ⅓ cup pistachios, finely chopped
> 1 teaspoon grated lemon zest
> ¼ cup fresh lemon juice
> 2 garlic cloves, minced
> 1 teaspoon chopped fresh thyme
> ½ teaspoon salt plus more to taste
> ¼ teaspoon pepper plus more to taste
> 4 center-cut pork chops, 1¼ inch thick
> Extra-virgin olive oil to coat

Soak plank according to instructions on page xix.

To make stuffing, combine bread crumbs, pistachios, lemon zest, lemon juice, garlic, thyme, salt, and pepper in a medium bowl. If the stuffing feels a little dry, add 1 to 2 tablespoons water to moisten.

Slice pork chops in half toward the bone, creating a pocket. Spoon about 2 tablespoons stuffing into the pocket of each chop. Brush both sides of pork chops with olive oil and season with salt and pepper.

Prepare plank for grilling according to instructions on page xx. Place chops on plank. Close lid and grill for 20 minutes or until meat thermometer registers 150 degrees F. Allow pork chops to rest for 5 minutes before serving.

MAKES 4 SERVINGS

Apple Pecan Stuffed Pork Chops

by: **MICHELLE LOWREY**

PLANK PREFERENCE: **ALL**

Sunday dinner at our house was always a big deal growing up. Right after the breakfast dishes were cleared, my mom would start planning the big meal of the day, which would take place about four or five o'clock in the afternoon. My sister Anna and I were taught "to act like respectful young ladies," and when my grandpa was dining with us, heaven forbid you had your elbows on the table! My mom was insistent on those Sunday dinners, and as I got older I dreaded having to stop my activities that seemed so much more important than dinner. As an adult I am so thankful for not only the wonderful meals she so lovingly prepared, but the family bonds that were created and that will never be broken. Stuffed pork chops were a Sunday staple that I now make for my own family. The grilling plank is perfect for keeping the juices inside the meat, and it helps to keep the pork from drying out.

3 slices pepper bacon
¼ cup diced celery
¼ cup diced onion
3 tablespoons unsalted butter
¼ cup chopped pecans
½ cup peeled and diced apple
1 teaspoon nutmeg
1 tablespoon fresh thyme, or 1 teaspoon dried
1 teaspoon dried sage
1 cup fresh, cubed bread
Water as needed
4 center-cut pork chops, 1¼ inch thick
Salt and pepper to taste

Soak plank according to instructions on page xix.

To make stuffing, fry bacon in a large skillet until crisp and set aside. In the same skillet, add celery and onion to bacon drippings and cook over medium heat until celery is tender but crisp, about 3 minutes. Melt butter into onion-and-celery mixture, then add pecans, apple, nutmeg, and herbs. Sauté for 3 to 4 minutes and remove from heat.

Crumble reserved bacon. Add bread and bacon to onion-and-celery mixture and mix well. Add water, a little at a time, if mixture becomes too dry. Set stuffing aside.

Slice pork chops in half toward the bone, creating a pocket, and spread liberally with salt and pepper inside and out. Fill pockets with stuffing.

Prepare plank for grilling according to instructions on page xx. Place chops on plank. Close lid and grill for 18 to 20 minutes over low heat, or until chops come to an internal temperature of 150 degrees F. Remove pork chops from grill and transfer to serving platter. Cover with foil and allow to rest for 5 minutes before serving.

MAKES 4 SERVINGS

Pork Chops *with* Honey Balsamic Glaze

by: MICHELLE LOWREY

PLANK PREFERENCE: **ALL**

This recipe was created when I couldn't think of what to prepare for dinner and the cupboards were pretty bare. I threw together some honey and balsamic vinegar with a few spices and marinated some pork chops, not sure what to expect. Well, not only were these a hit, but they are probably one of my favorite ways to prepare pork now. Simple ingredients are always the best, and this is the recipe my family will ask for if they know pork is on the menu. These sweet, succulent chops hit your taste buds in just the right spot.

¼ **cup balsamic vinegar**
¼ **cup honey**
2 teaspoons salt
¼ **teaspoon dried thyme**
3 garlic cloves, minced
Dash crushed red pepper (optional)
4 center-cut pork chops, 1 inch thick

Soak plank according to instructions on page xix.

To make the glaze, in a small bowl combine the vinegar, honey, salt, thyme, garlic, and crushed red pepper, if using. Put pork chops into large glass baking dish and pour the glaze over the pork chops. Coat chops well and refrigerate for 2 hours.

Bring chops to room temperature. Drain excess glaze into a small saucepan and reserve.

Prepare plank for grilling according to instructions on page xx. Place chops on plank. Close lid and grill for 14 to 16 minutes, or until chops reach an internal temperature of 150 degrees F. Remove chops from grill, place on platter, and cover with foil. Allow to sit for 5 minutes.

During the last few minutes of grilling time, bring reserved glaze to a boil and thicken slightly, about 2 to 3 minutes. Pour glaze over chops after they have rested and serve immediately.

MAKES 4 SERVINGS

Orange *and* Sesame Pork Tenderloin

by: **MARIA EVERLY**

PLANK PREFERENCE: **ALL**

The toasted sesame oil, orange juice, orange zest, and soy sauce add both Asian character and flavor to the mild pork. The grilling plank infuses a delicious smoky flavor and transforms the marinade into a glaze, which settles beautifully over the tenderloin. The meat will be incredibly moist and succulent. Save any leftovers for sandwiches the next day.

> 1- to 2-pound pork tenderloin, or two 1-pound tenderloins
> Zest of 1 medium orange
> Juice of 1 medium orange
> 1 medium shallot, finely diced
> 4 garlic cloves, diced
> ⅓ cup soy sauce
> ¾ cup extra-virgin olive oil
> 1 tablespoon toasted sesame oil
> ¼ cup brown sugar
> 2 tablespoons garlic powder
> Small bunch fresh rosemary
> Small bunch fresh thyme

Soak plank according to instructions on page xix.

Wash tenderloin and pat dry with paper towels. Set aside.

To make the marinade, in a small bowl combine the orange zest, orange juice, shallot, garlic, soy sauce, olive oil, sesame oil, brown sugar, garlic powder, rosemary, and thyme. Mix well. Put marinade and tenderloin in a large resealable plastic bag and lock seal. Gently move tenderloin around so meat is completely covered with marinade. Marinate in refrigerator at least 8 hours or overnight. Turn bag over a couple of times if possible.

Remove tenderloin from bag. Put on large plate and allow to warm to room temperature, about 30 minutes.

Prepare plank for grilling according to instructions on page xx. Place tenderloin on plank. Close lid and grill for about 20 minutes, or until meat is no longer pink in the center. Meat thermometer should read between 150 and 160 degrees F. Remove meat from grill and allow to rest for about 5 minutes. Cut into desired thickness and serve.

MAKES 4 TO 6 SERVINGS

Juniper *and* Porcini Lamb Chops

by: DINA GUILLEN

PLANK PREFERENCE: **ALL**

Juniper berries are probably best known as the flavoring agent in gin, but they are not just good for making martinis. Juniper berries are also used in cooking venison, duck, boar, hare, and other game. The berries are usually crushed to release their flavor and added to soups, sauces, or marinades. In this recipe, I decided to make a rub out of the berries since they have a slight overtone of pine flavor that goes so well with the earthiness of the mushrooms. You can find juniper berries in the spice section of specialty food markets. This recipe also calls for crumbled dried porcini mushrooms that will be ground into a powder. The best way to crumble the dried mushrooms is to take the dried mushroom pieces and just crumble them with your fingers over a cookie sheet.

> 2 level tablespoons crumbled dried porcini mushrooms
> 1 tablespoon dried juniper berries, ground
> ½ teaspoon salt
> ¼ teaspoon pepper
> Eight 4-ounce lamb rib chops, trimmed

Soak plank according to instructions on page xix.

Put mushrooms in a spice or coffee grinder, and process until finely ground. The ground mushroom powder should yield 1 tablespoon. In a small bowl, combine mushroom powder, juniper berries, salt, and pepper, reserving the remaining ground mushrooms for another use.

Rub lamb chops with mushroom mixture. Set aside.

Prepare plank for grilling according to instructions on page xx. Place chops on plank. Close lid and grill for 15 minutes, or until thermometer registers 140 degrees F for medium rare. Allow chops to sit for 5 minutes before serving.

MAKES 4 SERVINGS

Curry and Ginger Lamb Chops *with* Spicy Peach Sauce

by: DINA GUILLEN

PLANK PREFERENCE: **ALL**

My husband, Roland, is not a big fan of lamb, and unfortunately for him he married into a lamb-lovin' family. Whenever there is a big celebration in my family, an entire lamb is served. At small gatherings, there is just a leg of lamb, or lamb kebabs, or lamb burgers. My family does not know about Roland's dislike of lamb because he is so gracious about it (if they are reading this, I guess they just found out), so when I created this dish, I assumed Roland was being gracious again when he finished his plate and proclaimed it a winner. But he has asked for this dish several times since then, and I am glad to have converted him to our side. The sweetness from the preserves works beautifully in this dish with the tanginess of the curry and the smoke-infused lamb. If you do not have peach preserves, you can substitute apricot preserves.

> 1-inch piece fresh ginger, peeled, cut into fourths
> 1½ tablespoons curry powder
> 3 shallots
> ¼ cup extra-virgin olive oil
> 4 lamb shoulder chops, ¾ inch thick
> 2 cups Spicy Peach Sauce (recipe follows)

Soak plank according to instructions on page xix.

In a food processor or blender, purée ginger, curry powder, shallots, and olive oil until smooth. Brush evenly over lamb chops.

Prepare plank for grilling according to instructions on page xx. Place lamb on plank. Close lid and grill 15 minutes on one side. Turn lamb, brush with half of Spicy Peach Sauce, close lid, and grill 5 minutes. Turn lamb, brush with remaining Spicy Peach Sauce, close lid, and grill another 5 minutes, or until thermometer registers 140 degrees F for medium rare. Remove from plank and allow to rest for 5 minutes before serving.

MAKES 4 SERVINGS

SPICY PEACH SAUCE

⅔ cup peach preserves
½ cup fresh lime juice
¼ cup ketchup
⅓ cup chopped fresh mint
¼ cup soy sauce
⅛ teaspoon cayenne
¼ teaspoon salt
¼ teaspoon pepper

Melt preserves in a small saucepan over medium-low heat until syrupy. Stir in remaining ingredients. Remove from heat.

MAKES 2 CUPS

Sizzling Lamb Fajitas

by: **DINA GUILLEN**

PLANK PREFERENCE: **ALL**

Fajitas *are traditionally prepared with skirt steak and grilled over hot coals. In fact,* fajita *actually means "grilled skirt steak." So, while purists may object to this recipe being called "lamb fajitas," the fun part of cooking is trying your own versions of dishes that are popular. Plank-grilling the meat takes fajitas to another level that just bursts with flavor. I love the taste of lamb grilled on the plank, but this dish can easily be made with the traditional skirt steak or with chicken, pork, shrimp, or just vegetables. They are all delicious served with a lot of condiments on the side.*

¼ cup plus 2 tablespoons extra-virgin olive oil
¼ cup orange juice
½ cup fresh lime juice
Zest of 1 lime
1 jalapeño, seeded and minced
½ cup cilantro, chopped
1 tablespoon chili powder
1 teaspoon oregano
1 teaspoon ground cumin
1 teaspoon onion powder
1 teaspoon garlic powder
½ teaspoon cayenne
One 2-pound boneless leg of lamb, butterflied
Salt and pepper
1 large red onion, cut into 1-inch-thick slices
2 large bell peppers, red or green or one of each, cut into ½-inch-
    thick slices
Salt and pepper
12 tortillas, warmed
Sour cream, guacamole, cilantro sprigs, and lime wedges for garnish

Soak plank according to instructions on page xix.

In a medium bowl, combine the ¼ cup olive oil, orange juice, lime juice, lime zest, jalapeño, cilantro, and spices and mix well. Pour marinade over meat in a shallow, nonreactive container or resealable plastic bag. Refrigerate overnight or up to 24 hours.

Prepare plank for grilling according to instructions on page xx. Drain the marinade from the lamb, season with salt and pepper, and place lamb on plank. Close lid and grill for 40 minutes, or until the thermometer registers 140 degrees F for medium-rare. Allow lamb to rest for 10 minutes before cutting diagonally into finger-length strips.

While lamb is grilling, heat remaining olive oil in a large skillet over medium-high heat. Add onion slices and cook 3 minutes. Stir in bell pepper strips and cook 1 minute. Season with salt and pepper, remove from pan, and keep warm.

Place lamb and vegetables in a warm tortilla and top with sour cream, guacamole, and sprigs of cilantro. Serve with lime wedges.

MAKES 6 SERVINGS

Rack *of* Lamb *over* Rosemary Pomegranate Sauce

by: DINA GUILLEN

PLANK PREFERENCE: **ALL**

It used to be that you could only find pomegranate juice in Middle Eastern grocery stores, but it is now more readily available in local supermarkets. You can, however, substitute any unsweetened dark juice, such as cranberry, cranberry-apple, currant, grape, or even prune. If you do use pomegranate juice, this dish looks very festive garnished with pomegranate seeds when they are in season.

> 8-rib rack of lamb, 1¼ to 1½ pounds
> 1½ cups pomegranate juice
> ¾ cup dry red wine
> 2 tablespoons extra-virgin olive oil
> 1 sprig fresh rosemary, leaves removed
> 1 shallot, minced
> 2 tablespoons butter
> ¼ cup lemon juice
> 1 cup beef broth
> 2 tablespoons seedless raspberry jam
> 1 teaspoon Dijon mustard
> 1 teaspoon chopped fresh rosemary
> 1 teaspoon chopped fresh thyme
> Salt and pepper
> Rosemary sprigs for garnish

Soak plank according to instructions on page xix.

Trim all visible fat from lamb. Set lamb aside.

To make the marinade, combine ½ cup pomegranate juice, ¼ cup wine, olive oil, and leaves from 1 rosemary sprig in a large glass baking dish, and add lamb. Marinate for several hours or overnight, turning occasionally. Discard marinade.

To make the sauce, in a large skillet sauté shallot in butter over medium heat until shallot is translucent. Add the remaining pomegranate juice, lemon juice, broth, remaining wine, jam, mustard, rosemary, and thyme, and cook until reduced by half and almost syrupy, about 20 minutes. Season with salt and pepper and set aside.

Prepare plank for grilling according to instructions on page xx. Place lamb on plank. Close lid, and grill for 20 minutes, or until thermometer registers 140 degrees F for medium-rare. Remove from grill and allow to rest for 5 minutes in a warm place. Cut lamb in double chops. To serve, spoon sauce onto individual serving plates, place lamb chops on top, and garnish with rosemary.

MAKES 4 SERVINGS

Lamb *and* Potato Kebabs

by: DINA GUILLEN

PLANK PREFERENCE: **ALL**

I love Mediterranean food, so I created this recipe using ingredients that are typical *of that cuisine. Try serving these kebabs with pita bread and a tossed green salad dressed with a simple lemon juice and extra-virgin olive oil dressing. If you are using wooden skewers, be sure to soak them in water for at least 30 minutes before placing on the grill.*

6 garlic cloves, minced
¾ cup finely chopped onion
½ cup dry red wine
¼ cup red wine vinegar
¼ cup extra-virgin olive oil
1 tablespoon Dijon mustard
Juice and zest of 1 large lemon
1 pound boneless leg of lamb, trimmed and cut into 16 one-inch
    cubes
6 small red potatoes, halved
1 tablespoon chopped fresh rosemary, or 1 teaspoon dried
1 teaspoon ground cumin
1 teaspoon salt
¼ teaspoon freshly ground black pepper
1 small onion, cut into wedges
4 skewers

Soak plank according to instructions on page xix.

To make the marinade, combine the garlic, onion, wine, vinegar, olive oil, mustard, and lemon juice in a large resealable plastic bag. Add lamb to bag, seal, and marinate in refrigerator for 2 to 12 hours, turning bag occasionally.

Remove lamb from bag and discard marinade. Put lamb in a large bowl and set aside. Put potatoes in a large saucepan, cover with water, and bring to a boil. Reduce heat and simmer for 10 minutes, or until barely tender. Drain and set aside.

Add lemon zest, rosemary, cumin, salt, and pepper to lamb. Toss gently to coat. Thread lamb, potato halves, and onion wedges alternately onto skewers.

Prepare plank for grilling according to instructions on page xx. Place kebabs on plank. Close lid and grill for 4 minutes on each side, or until lamb reaches desired degree of doneness. Remove from grill and allow to rest for 5 minutes before serving.

MAKES 4 SERVINGS

Fish *and* Shellfish

Salmon Filets *in a* Mustard Herb Crust

Mexican Fiesta Salmon Tacos

Salmon Filets *with* Butter, Shallot, *and* Fig Sauce

Maple Apricot Glazed Salmon *with* Sautéed Peaches
    and Pears

Salmon Filets *with* Mango, Peach, *and* Pineapple Salsa

Salmon Filet Sandwich

Red Snapper Soft Tacos

Tuna *with* Hoisin Sherry Sauce

Halibut *with* Fire-Roasted Tomato, Caper, *and*
    Artichoke Sauce

Halibut Wrapped *in* Grape Leaves *with* Lemon Caper Sauce

Tilapia Filets *with* Mashed Potatoes, Fried Leeks, *and*
    Lemon Pesto Butter Sauce

Melon Honey Prawns

Asian Shrimp *in* Lettuce Wraps

Rum Shrimp

Spicy Shrimp

Shrimp Wrapped *in* Bacon *over* Greens

Calamari Steaks *on* Mizuna

Lobster Tails *with* Orange Brandy Butter

Sea Scallops Wrapped *in* Pancetta *with* Asparagus *and*
    Cherry Tomatoes

Clams *and* Mussels *with* Basil *and* Tomato Salsa

The grilling plank has sparked a true transformation in the way we grill fish and shellfish. Not only have we discovered the impact the moist wood smoke has in creating sumptuous meals, we learned the versatility and simplicity of plank grilling. Needless to say, the grilling plank complements seafood and shellfish perfectly.

Although salmon is considered the king of the plank, you will be surprised at how extraordinarily moist, tender, and flavorful all of your other seafood dishes will be. We share here simple recipes such as *Calamari Steaks on Mizuna* (page 88) and *Melon Honey Prawns* (page 82), as well as elegant dishes such as *Lobster Tails with Orange Brandy Butter* (page 90) and *Salmon Filets with Butter, Shallot, and Fig Sauce* (page 65). For a little more time and effort, you will be rewarded with *Tilapia Filets with Mashed Potatoes, Fried Leeks, and Lemon Pesto Butter Sauce* (page 80).

Hors d'oeuvres such as the *Rum Shrimp* (page 85) or *Sea Scallops Wrapped in Pancetta with Asparagus and Cherry Tomatoes* (page 92) will get your dinner party or special occasion off to a delicious beginning. With wonderful tastes and beautiful presentation, the grilling plank truly gives fish and shellfish the best of what grilling has to offer.

Salmon Filets *in a* Mustard Herb Crust

by: MICHELLE LOWREY

PLANK PREFERENCE: **CEDAR**

I see plank-grilled salmon on more and more restaurant menus, and the appeal is universal. Try to find salmon filets that are uniform in thickness for even cooking. Keep a water bottle handy, as flare-ups can happen, but try to keep the grill lid closed to get as much smoke flavor as possible infused into the fish. Lastly, any bread crumbs will work fine, but I like the taste and texture of panko (coarse Japanese bread crumbs) the best.

Four 6-ounce salmon filets
½ cup mayonnaise
½ small lemon, juiced
¼ cup snipped fresh dill, or 2 teaspoons dried
¼ cup whole-grain mustard
½ teaspoon salt
¼ teaspoon ground black pepper
1 cup unseasoned panko
Lemon wedges for garnish

Soak plank according to instructions on page xix.

Rinse salmon filets well and pat dry with paper towels. Set aside.

To make the mustard crust, in a small bowl combine mayonnaise, lemon juice, dill, mustard, salt, and pepper. Mix well. Spread mustard mixture evenly over salmon filets and sprinkle liberally with bread crumbs to form a thick, even coating. With your fingers, lightly press crumbs into salmon so they adhere well.

Prepare plank for grilling according to instructions on page xx. Place salmon filets on plank, skin side down. Close lid and grill until crispy on the surface but still moist and slightly opaque in the center, about 18 to 20 minutes depending on thickness of fish. Remove skin before serving and garnish with lemon wedges.

MAKES 4 SERVINGS

Mexican Fiesta Salmon Tacos

by: **MICHELLE LOWREY**

PLANK PREFERENCE: **ALL**

This recipe is so easy and is great for a night on the backyard patio. I usually like to use fresh herbs whenever possible, but in this particular recipe the dried herbs work better for seasoning the fish. The dry ingredients can be used as liberally as you like; simply store any unused portion in an airtight container up to three months.

1-pound salmon filet, skin attached
2 tablespoons chili powder
1 tablespoon salt
2 teaspoons granulated garlic powder
2 teaspoons ground cumin
1 teaspoon ground black pepper
1 teaspoon dried oregano
1 teaspoon cayenne
¼ teaspoon ground coriander
¼ teaspoon ground cloves
1 cup sour cream
1 tablespoon milk
¼ cup good quality salsa
½ medium green cabbage, cut into thin wedges
2 limes, cut into quarters
8 corn tortillas, warmed

Soak plank according to instructions on page xix.

Rinse salmon filet and dry well with paper towels. Set aside.

Mix all dry ingredients in small bowl until well combined. Rub liberally onto flesh side of salmon and put salmon in refrigerator for 1 hour.

Prepare plank for grilling according to instructions on page xx. Place salmon on plank, skin side up. Close lid and grill 20 minutes, or until salmon is flaky around edges but still opaque in the center. Carefully remove skin and cut into 8 serving pieces. Transfer to serving platter.

To serve, combine the sour cream, milk, and salsa in a small bowl to make the fish sauce. Offer plenty of sliced cabbage, lime wedges, warmed tortillas, and sauce with the salmon.

MAKES 8 TACOS

Salmon Filets *with* Butter, Shallot, *and* Fig Sauce

by: MARIA EVERLY

PLANK PREFERENCE: **ALDER**

Ihave been blessed with the gift of great friends. I met Dina through the cooking club and was immediately drawn to her. Dina introduced me to the joys of cooking with figs. This dish combines great taste and an elegant presentation and was inspired by this superclassy and amazing friend. Plank-grilled salmon alone is divine, but when topped with this butter-fig sauce the taste is simply exquisite. Biting into the silky, velvety texture of a plank-grilled fig is a rich and sweet sensation not to be missed. This will be a recipe you will make over and over again.

> Four 6- to 8-ounce salmon filets
> Salt and pepper
> 8 dried figs
> ¼ cup butter
> ¼ cup finely diced shallots
> ¼ cup orange juice
> ½ cup dried fig jam or preserves (such as Dalmatia
>   Dried Fig Spread)
> 5 whole jumbo shelled walnuts, chopped (optional)

Soak plank according to instructions on page xix.

Rinse salmon with cold water, pat dry with paper towels, and season with salt and pepper. Set aside.

In a small bowl, soak the dried figs in hot water for 30 minutes. Drain, thinly slice, and set aside.

To make the sauce, in a medium saucepan melt butter over low heat. Raise heat to medium, add shallots, and sauté for about 4 minutes or until soft. Add orange juice, fig spread, and figs. Mix until all ingredients are combined.

Remove from heat. Pour sauce over salmon filets and set aside.

Prepare plank for grilling according to instructions on page xx. Place salmon filets on plank. Close lid and grill for about 15 minutes, or until fish begins to flake. Remove fish from grill and allow to rest for 3 to 5 minutes. Sprinkle with walnuts and serve.

MAKES 4 SERVINGS

Maple Apricot Glazed Salmon *with* Sautéed Peaches *and* Pears

by: MARIA EVERLY

PLANK PREFERENCE: **CEDAR**

I have been lucky enough to experience New England in the fall. The awe and feeling of being surrounded by an abundant number of rich and radiant colors is indescribable. The colors and taste of New England are well represented in this recipe. The sauce pulls all the great flavors together, and the cedar plank responds by bringing out the richness of the sweet and buttery combination. The maple syrup and preserves caramelize during the grilling process. The result is a beautiful luminous crimson glaze over the top of the salmon. If you would like to enjoy this dish with a glass of wine, try a light-bodied wine such as chardonnay or Riesling.

> Four 6- to 8-ounce salmon filets or steaks
> Salt and pepper
> Dried ground ginger
> ¼ cup maple syrup
> ¼ cup apricot preserves (such as Bonne Maman)
> 1½ tablespoons brown sugar
> 1 teaspoon coarse-grain mustard
> 1½ tablespoons orange juice
> 2 tablespoons butter
> 2 fresh marjoram sprigs, plucked
> 2 tablespoons sliced almonds
> 1 semifirm peach, peeled and thinly sliced
> 1 Red Bartlett pear, or any red pear, peeled and thinly sliced
> 1 tablespoon balsamic vinegar

Soak plank according to instructions on page xix.

Rinse salmon and pat dry with paper towels. Place in a large shallow baking dish or on a platter. Season with salt, pepper, and a dash of ginger. Set aside.

In a medium bowl, combine maple syrup, apricot preserves, brown sugar, mustard, and orange juice. Mix well and pour over salmon filets. Make sure apricot-preserve chunks rest on top of each filet. Set aside.

Prepare plank for grilling according to instructions on page xx. Place salmon filets on plank. Close lid and grill for about 15 minutes, or until fish begins to flake.

While fish is grilling, prepare fruit. In a medium nonstick pan, melt butter over medium-high heat. When butter turns lightly brown add marjoram and almonds, and sauté for 1 minute. Add the peach and pear slices and balsamic vinegar. Sauté for about 2 minutes. Add salt to taste.

Remove fish from grill and allow to rest for 5 minutes. Place one filet on each plate and evenly distribute the fruit sauté over the filets.

MAKES 4 SERVINGS

Salmon Filets *with* Mango, Peach, *and* Pineapple Salsa

by: MARIA EVERLY

PLANK PREFERENCE: CEDAR

I am a big fan of the Caribbean islands. To me, they are the closest thing to paradise. This tropical salsa and salmon recipe puts the tropics on display. The tropical fruit salsa is a melody of fruits and juices, best prepared with the freshest ingredients available. Each bite is a delicious blend of sweet, tangy, and crunchy textures and tastes. The honey, butter, and oranges bring out the richer tones in the salmon, and the cedar plank complements it by finishing it with a subtle smoky taste. The result is a sweet, mouthwatering experience with no need to travel to the islands.

¾ cup finely diced pineapple
½ cup finely diced mango
½ cup finely diced peach
¼ cup finely diced red bell pepper
¼ cup finely diced red onion
1 tablespoon chopped fresh cilantro
1 tablespoon orange juice
2 tablespoons fresh lime juice
Salt and pepper
Four 6- to 8-ounce salmon filets or steak
All-purpose season salt
2 teaspoons honey
4 tablespoons unsalted butter, divided
4 finely chopped green onions
1 medium orange, cut into 8 slices

Soak plank according to instructions on page xix.

To make the salsa, in a medium bowl combine the pineapple, mango, peach, bell pepper, red onion, cilantro, and both juices. Lightly toss and season with salt and pepper to taste. Cover and refrigerate for up to 1 hour.

Rinse salmon and pat dry with paper towels. Place salmon filets skin side down on a large, shallow platter and season with salt, pepper, and season salt. Drizzle ½ teaspoon honey over each filet. Place 1 tablespoon butter on each filet. Sprinkle filets with green onions and top each with 2 orange slices. Set aside.

Prepare plank for grilling according to instructions on page xx. Place salmon filets on plank. Close lid and grill for about 10 to 12 minutes, or until fish begins to flake. Remove fish from grill and allow to rest for 5 minutes.

Remove orange slices. Spoon salsa on the side or on top of filets and serve.

MAKES 4 SERVINGS

Lemon Herb Roast Chicken ~ *page 5*

Pork Baby Back Ribs *with* Sweet Barbecue Sauce ~ *page 40*

Apple Pecan Stuffed Pork Chops ~ *page 43*

Maple Apricot Glazed Salmon *with* Sautéed Peaches *and* Pears ~ *page 67*

Corn *on the* Cob ~ *page 97*

Tilapia Filets *with* Mashed Potatoes, Fried Leeks, *and* Lemon Pesto Butter Sauce, *page 80*

Clams *and* Mussels *with* Basil *and* Tomato Salsa ~ *page 94*

Strawberries *with* Lemon Cream Parfait ~ *page 127*

Peaches *with* Crème Fraîche Topping ~ *page* 129

Salmon Filet Sandwich

by: **MARIA EVERLY**

PLANK PREFERENCE: **CEDAR**

My twist on a club sandwich, this dish is anything but ordinary. Although it may appear fancy, it is easy to prepare and assemble. The plank spikes up the flavor, while the filets remain moist and tender on the grill. If you cannot locate lemon tartar sauce, add 1 tablespoon fresh lemon juice to regular tartar sauce. This dish pairs well with a pasta salad.

Four 6- to 8-ounce salmon filets
Salt and pepper
¼ cup extra-virgin olive oil
2 lemons
12 pancetta slices, or 8 bacon slices
¼ cup lemon tartar sauce
2 teaspoons capers, drained
¼ to ½ cup mayonnaise
8 slices sourdough bread, or any hearty bread
4 slices store-bought roasted red bell pepper (such as Divina)
2 medium tomatoes, cut into ¼-inch diagonal slices
2 cups mesclun salad mix
Salt and pepper
Fresh basil leaves (optional)

Soak plank according to instructions on page xix.

Rinse salmon and pat dry with paper towels. Place filets in a large, shallow baking dish or on a platter, skin side down. Season with salt and pepper and set aside.

In a small bowl, whisk together olive oil and juice from one lemon. Pour over filets and set aside.

Prepare plank for grilling according to instructions on page xx. Place salmon filets on plank, skin side down. Close lid, and grill for about 15 minutes, or until fish begins to flake.

While fish is grilling, fry pancetta for about 8 to 10 minutes. Remove from heat and drain on a plate lined with paper towels. Set aside.

In a small bowl, combine tartar sauce and capers.

Remove fish from grill. Spread 1 tablespoon of tartar caper sauce over each filet. Allow to rest for 5 minutes.

While fish is resting, toast bread. Spread desired amount of mayonnaise on each slice of toasted bread. Place 1 filet on 1 piece of bread, squeeze the remaining lemon and sprinkle filet with juice, and season with salt and pepper. Layer pancetta, roasted red peppers, tomatoes, mesclun, and optional basil. Top with remaining bread slice and enjoy!

MAKES 4 SANDWICHES

Red Snapper Soft Tacos

by: **MARIA EVERLY**

PLANK PREFERENCE: **CEDAR**

Brought up in Southern California, I have fond memories of driving to the local taco stand and eating fish tacos by the half dozen. This simple and tasty meal is a great variation of a traditional fish taco recipe. It was inspired by my childhood and is a gift to my sister, who loves fish tacos so much that she has been known to drive more than a hundred miles to satisfy her craving. Kid-friendly and yummy too!

1 pound red snapper filets
One 12- to 16-ounce jar of salsa (roasted tomato, mild Southwest, or
    peach are recommended)
Six 6-inch flour tortillas, warmed
¼ of a medium cabbage, shredded
6 tablespoons sour cream
2 limes, each cut into 4 slices
Shredded lettuce (optional)
1 lemon, cut into 4 slices (optional)
Chopped tomatoes (optional)
Grated cheddar cheese (optional)

Soak plank according to instructions on page xix.

Put filets in a large resealable plastic bag, pour salsa over fish, and lock seal. Gently move bag around to coat fish. Put in refrigerator and marinate 2 to 8 hours. If possible turn bag over periodically. Remove filets from bag, place on platter, and allow to warm to room temperature, about 30 minutes.

Prepare plank for grilling according to instructions on page xx. Place red snapper on plank. Close lid and grill for about 15 minutes, or until fish begins to flake. Remove fish from grill and allow to rest for 3 to 5 minutes.

Now the fun part begins! Fill each warm tortilla with some fish, cabbage, and sour cream. Squeeze a lime slice over the taco and enjoy! Feel free to substitute any of the optional ingredients.

MAKES 6 TACOS

Tuna *with* **Hoisin Sherry Sauce**

by: **DINA GUILLEN**

PLANK PREFERENCE: **CEDAR**

One of my favorite pastimes is entertaining at home with good friends and good food. I think that combination, friends and food, is why I have enjoyed the process of writing this cookbook so much. There are very few things better than having friends within hugging distance and sharing a good meal together. I will often create a dish and invite friends over to try it. This recipe came about during one of those "creative" sessions and it ended up turning into a big hit. I love the sauce in this recipe because it has such a range of flavors—spicy, sweet, sour, smoky, and woody. I have used the leftover sauce produced by this recipe with plank-grilled butterflied pork tenderloin and a whole chicken split in half, basting with the sauce in the last 10 minutes of grilling time.

> **Four 6-ounce tuna steaks**
> **Coarse salt and freshly ground pepper**
> **Hoisin Sherry Sauce (recipe follows)**

Soak plank according to instructions on page xix.

Sprinkle tuna steaks with salt and pepper.

Prepare plank for grilling according to instructions on page xx. Over medium-high heat, place tuna steaks on plank. Close lid and grill for 10 minutes. Turn tuna over and baste with a thin layer of sauce. Close lid and cook for 3 minutes. Turn tuna over and baste the other side with sauce. Close lid and cook for 2 minutes, or until tuna flakes easily when tested with a fork. Store unused portion of sauce in the refrigerator for later use.

MAKES 4 SERVINGS

HOISIN SHERRY SAUCE

2 tablespoons peanut or corn oil
2 large shallots, coarsely chopped
4 large garlic cloves, minced
1 tablespoon peeled and grated ginger
One 14½-ounce can diced tomatoes
½ cup hoisin sauce
¼ cup sugar
2 tablespoons soy sauce
¼ cup rice wine vinegar
1 tablespoon chili sauce with garlic
¼ cup dry sherry

Heat oil in a medium saucepan over medium-high heat. Add shallots, garlic, and ginger, and cook until soft, about 4 minutes. Add the remaining ingredients, bring to a boil, and cook for 3 minutes. Remove from heat and allow to cool for 20 minutes. Transfer to a blender and blend until smooth.

MAKES ABOUT 3½ CUPS

Halibut *with* Fire-Roasted Tomato, Caper, *and* Artichoke Sauce

by: MARIA EVERLY

PLANK PREFERENCE: **ALDER**

Rich alder smoke adds a succulent taste to the light and flaky halibut, and the concentrated flavors of the fire-roasted tomatoes impart a robust flavor to this simple and delicious sauce. The halibut and sauce together form an irresistible combination, boasting both sweet and mild flavors. The beauty of this sauce is that it can be made up to three days ahead and makes more than enough for leftovers the next day. Try it served over pasta, sea bass, red snapper, or scallops.

¼ cup butter
4 teaspoons lemon juice
1 teaspoon garlic salt
½ teaspoon lemon pepper
Four 6- to 8-ounce halibut filets
2 cups Fire-Roasted Tomato, Caper, and Artichoke Sauce
   (recipe follows)

Soak plank according to instructions on page xix.

Melt butter in a small saucepan on the stovetop, or microwave in a microwave-safe dish. Remove from heat and add lemon juice, garlic salt, and lemon pepper. Mix well and brush butter sauce over filets.

Prepare plank for grilling according to instructions on page xx. Place halibut on plank. Close lid and grill for about 15 minutes, or until fish flakes easily when tested with a fork. Remove fish from grill and allow to cool for 3 to 5 minutes. Pour ½ cup of warm sauce over each fish filet, or serve on the side.

MAKES 4 SERVINGS

FIRE-ROASTED TOMATO, CAPER, *and* ARTICHOKE SAUCE

One 28-ounce can fire-roasted diced tomatoes in juice (substitute
    regular diced tomatoes if fire-roasted are not available)
¼ cup extra-virgin olive oil
½ cup finely chopped white onion
2 large garlic cloves, finely chopped
2 tablespoons snipped fresh dill
¼ cup finely chopped fresh basil
1 teaspoon dried oregano
½ cup marinated artichoke hearts, drained and chopped
3 tablespoons drained capers
Salt and pepper

Put tomatoes in a fine sieve over a bowl. With a spoon or potato masher, press tomatoes against sieve to further separate juice from tomatoes. You want to slightly crush the tomatoes as the juice is being pressed out. Reserve the juice in bowl, and set aside crushed tomatoes.

Heat olive oil in a large, heavy skillet over medium-high heat. Add onion and sauté for 1 minute. Add garlic and sauté for another minute. Add crushed tomatoes to onions and garlic and cook for 2 minutes. Add dill, basil, oregano, and ¼ cup of reserved tomato juice. Simmer about 3 to 4 minutes until juice evaporates. Add artichokes, capers, and remaining tomato juice. Add salt and pepper to taste. Stir occasionally and simmer about 10 minutes, or until sauce thickens. Cover and refrigerate until ready to use. Reheat before using.

MAKES ABOUT 3½ CUPS

Halibut Wrapped *in* Grape Leaves *with* Lemon Caper Sauce

by: DINA GUILLEN

PLANK PREFERENCE: **MAPLE**

Grilling grape leaves on a plank gives them the most delicious smoky caramel-ized flavor. This recipe works best with maplewood since it has a delicate smo-kiness that really complements the grape leaves and sauce in this dish. Any firm white fish can be substituted for the halibut, such as red snapper, bass, grouper, or swordfish. If you are using fresh grape leaves, it is important to remove the stems and blanch the leaves in boiling water for 5 minutes before wrapping them around the fish.

1 pound halibut filet
Salt and pepper
12 grape leaves brined in jar, rinsed and stemmed
⅓ cup extra-virgin olive oil
Zest of 2 large lemons
12 thin slices red onion
1 tablespoon chopped fresh flat-leaf parsley
1 tablespoon chopped fresh thyme
½ cup Lemon Caper Sauce (recipe follows)

Soak plank according to instructions on page xix.

Cut the fish into 12 pieces and season with salt and pepper. Fan grape leaves on a work surface, vein side (dull side) up. Put the olive oil in a medium shallow dish. Roll a piece of fish in oil, and place in the center of 1 grape leaf. Sprinkle a little zest on fish, place a slice of onion on top, and scatter a little parsley and thyme over the onion. Fold sides of leaf over fish, fold up bottom, and then con-tinue to roll up to make a neat roll. Repeat with remaining grape leaves. Place grape-leaf rolls back in dish with olive oil, brushing the outsides of the rolls with oil.

Prepare plank for grilling according to instructions on page xx. Place grape-leaf rolls seam side down on plank. Close lid and grill for 10 minutes.

Transfer grape-leaf rolls to serving plates and pour a little sauce over the top. The remaining sauce can be served on the side. Have guests unwrap the fish at the table, pour a little more sauce over fish, and invite them to eat the grape leaves with the fish.

MAKES 12 ROLLS

LEMON CAPER SAUCE

1 teaspoon chopped fresh thyme
2 tablespoons drained capers
3 tablespoons fresh lemon juice
⅓ cup extra-virgin olive oil
Salt and pepper

Whisk all ingredients together in a small bowl, season with salt and pepper to taste, and set aside.

MAKES ½ CUP

Tilapia Filets *with* Mashed Potatoes, Fried Leeks, *and* Lemon Pesto Butter Sauce

by: MARIA EVERLY

PLANK PREFERENCE: **ALL**

This recipe offers a unique contrast of crispy, creamy, and sweet textures. I love fish served over warm mashed potatoes. The buttery Yukon gold potatoes lend extra creaminess to the dish. The butter sauce is a perfect accompaniment because it enhances your palate, allowing your taste buds to distribute the wonderful blend of butter, pesto, and citrus juices. Substitute any mild, thin white fish if tilapia is not available.

    2 pounds Yukon gold potatoes, peeled and quartered
    1 cup milk
    11 tablespoons butter
    Salt and pepper
    3 tablespoons extra-virgin olive oil
    1 leek, cleaned and green part removed, cut into very thin strips
    1½ pounds tilapia filets
    3 garlic cloves, minced
    Zest of 1 large lemon
    ½ of 1 large lemon, juiced
    1 tablespoon orange juice
    ½ tablespoon basil pesto (such as Classico Creations)
    1 tablespoon chopped fresh flat-leaf parsley

Soak plank according to instructions on page xix.

To make the mashed potatoes, put potatoes in a large stockpot. Fill with cold water 2 inches above potatoes and bring to a boil. Reduce heat to medium-low, cover, and simmer until tender, about 25 minutes. Drain potatoes in colander. Squeeze one potato at a time through a potato ricer over a medium bowl. If potato ricer is not available, use a potato masher.

In a small saucepan, heat milk and 5 tablespoons of the butter, cut into chunks, over moderately low heat until butter is melted. Add the warm milk and butter mixture to potatoes and mix well. Season with salt and pepper to taste.

To make the fried leeks, in a medium skillet over high heat, heat olive oil until hot. Reduce heat to medium, add leek strips, and fry until lightly golden brown, about 5 minutes. Remove from skillet with slotted spoon and drain on paper towels. Set aside.

Prepare plank for grilling according to instructions on page xx. Season filets with salt and pepper. Place fish on plank. Close lid and grill for about 8 to 10 minutes, or until fish begins to flake.

Make the sauce while the fish is grilling. To make the sauce, in a small saucepan over medium to low heat, melt remaining butter. Add garlic and sauté about 1 minute. Add lemon zest, lemon juice, orange juice, pesto, and parsley. Stir gently. Reserve sauce on stove at lowest heat possible until ready to use.

Remove fish from grill and allow to rest for 5 minutes. Place a fourth of the potatoes in the middle of each plate, place a filet on the potatoes, and pour 2 tablespoons of butter sauce over each filet. Top with fried leeks.

MAKES 4 SERVINGS

Melon Honey Prawns

by: GRETCHEN BERNSDORFF

PLANK PREFERENCE: **MAPLE**

Prawns have always been my favorite seafood. As a matter of fact, I have eaten more than a pound of prawns in one sitting. I usually just eat my prawns plain, but the richness of this sauce is so scrumptious you will think you had dessert first. The sauce is very rich and creamy, but maintains a light feeling because of the fresh melon. Make this recipe as-is for an appetizer, or double the amounts and make it a meal. The sauce can also be used on kebabs made with chicken, pineapple, and red onions. Try plank-grilling the onions and pineapple, skewering them with chicken, and then drizzling with sauce.

¼ cup dry sherry
¼ cup red wine vinegar
½ cup honeydew melon (about ¼ of a small melon), puréed
½ pound fresh prawns, peeled and deveined
2 tablespoons extra-virgin olive oil
1 teaspoon dried ground ginger
6 tablespoons light mayonnaise
¼ cup honey
1½ tablespoons creamy peanut butter
½ small honeydew melon, cut into ½-inch cubes
½ small cantaloupe, cut into ½-inch cubes
3 tablespoons candied walnuts for garnish

Soak plank according to instructions on page xix.

To make the marinade, in a medium bowl whisk together the sherry, vinegar, melon purée, olive oil, and ginger. In a shallow baking dish, pour the marinade over prawns. Cover and refrigerate for at least 2 hours.

Prepare plank for grilling according to instructions on page xx. Place the prawns on the plank. Close lid and grill for 12 minutes, or until the prawns have turned pink. Be careful not to overcook. Prawns will become chewy if cooked too long.

To make the sauce, while the prawns are grilling combine mayonnaise, honey, and peanut butter in a small saucepan over medium heat. Stir constantly until a smooth, creamy consistency is achieved.

Just before removing the prawns from the grill, add the melon cubes to the sauce. Remove the prawns to a plate. Pour the sauce over the prawns and garnish with candied walnuts.

MAKES 2 SERVINGS

Asian Shrimp *in* Lettuce Wraps

by: DINA GUILLEN

PLANK PREFERENCE: **ALL**

T*his dish makes a nice appetizer. It is informal and easy and works well in a casual party setting where guests can gather and assemble their shrimp wraps while mingling. Assembling the wraps with a few sprigs of cilantro and toasted sesame seeds takes this dish over the top.*

1¼ cups plum sauce
¼ cup soy sauce
1 tablespoon sesame oil
1 teaspoon minced garlic
1 teaspoon minced ginger
½ teaspoon crushed red pepper
24 jumbo shrimp (about 2 pounds), peeled and deveined
1 cup cilantro sprigs
2 tablespoons toasted sesame seeds
Bibb lettuce for wrapping

Soak plank according to instructions on page xix.

To make the marinade, in a large, nonreactive bowl combine ¼ cup of the plum sauce, the soy sauce, sesame oil, garlic, ginger, and crushed red pepper and whisk well. Add the shrimp and toss to coat. Marinate in the refrigerator for 30 minutes.

Prepare plank for grilling according to instructions on page xx. Place shrimp on plank. If the shrimp are too large to all fit on one plank, prepare in two batches. It is important to not let them overlap. Close lid and grill for 5 minutes, or until the shrimp have turned pink. Be careful not to overcook. Shrimp will become chewy if cooked too long. Remove from grill. Put 2 to 3 shrimp, cilantro sprigs, a sprinkle of sesame seeds, and a drizzle of plum sauce on each lettuce leaf and wrap.

MAKES 12 WRAPS

Rum Shrimp

by: DINA GUILLEN

PLANK PREFERENCE: **ALL**

I t took me a long time to figure out that some of the best dishes are also some of the simplest dishes. When I graduated from college, I got a job at a television station producing public affairs talk shows. I was very excited about my new career and enjoyed putting in the hours. Even back then I had a zeal for learning how to cook and would come home late in the evening and actually begin making a dinner that required hours of preparation because I wanted a "good meal." If you do not have the time, or if you are new to plank grilling, this is a very simple and tasty dish to try. It makes a great appetizer, or you can serve it alongside a bed of rice garnished with coconut and mangoes to complete the tropical theme.

> 3 tablespoons rum
> 3 tablespoons honey
> 1 tablespoon teriyaki sauce
> 2 teaspoons Dijon mustard
> 1 teaspoon chili powder
> 24 large shrimp (about 2 pounds), peeled, with tails intact

Soak plank according to instructions on page xix.

To make the marinade, combine the rum, honey, teriyaki sauce, mustard, and chili powder in a large bowl and whisk together. Add shrimp to the rum mixture, tossing to coat. Marinate for 30 minutes.

Prepare plank for grilling according to instructions on page xx. Place shrimp on plank. Close lid and grill for 5 minutes, or until the shrimp have turned pink. Be careful not to overcook. Shrimp will become chewy if cooked too long.

MAKES 4 SERVINGS

Spicy Shrimp

by: DINA GUILLEN

PLANK PREFERENCE: **ALL**

Ilove the rub in this recipe because it can be used on just about anything, from shrimp to chicken to pork and even vegetables. It has a nice balance of sweet and spicy that works well with the smoke and wood. This dish makes a great appetizer for a party because it can be prepared quickly, leaving you time to enjoy being with your guests. Just serve with a simple dipping sauce of melted butter.

 1½ tablespoons sugar
 ½ tablespoon chili powder
 ½ teaspoon onion powder
 ½ teaspoon garlic powder
 ¼ teaspoon ground cumin
 ¼ teaspoon dried oregano
 ¼ teaspoon ground coriander
 ½ teaspoon coarse salt
 ¼ teaspoon freshly ground black pepper
 24 jumbo shrimp, (about 2 pounds) peeled and deveined
 ½ cup butter, melted

Soak plank according to instructions on page xix.

To make the shrimp rub, combine the sugar and spices in a small bowl. Sprinkle shrimp with spice rub and mix well. Set aside.

Prepare plank for grilling according to instructions on page xx. Place shrimp on plank. Close lid and grill for 5 minutes or until shrimp have turned pink. Be careful not to overcook. Shrimp will become chewy if cooked too long. Serve with melted butter as a dipping sauce.

MAKES 4 SERVINGS

Shrimp Wrapped *in* Bacon *over* Greens

by: MICHELLE LOWREY

PLANK PREFERENCE: **ALL**

This is such a summery salad, it begs to be served on the patio with cool glasses of sun tea. When coating the grilled shrimp with the vinaigrette mixture, leave the toothpicks in until ready to serve. That way the bacon will not fall off the shrimp, and the shrimp are much easier to find among the salad leaves.

> 2 heads butter lettuce
> 6 slices bacon, cut into thirds
> 16 jumbo shrimp (about 1 pound), peeled and deveined
> Garlic salt
> ¼ cup extra-virgin olive oil
> 2 tablespoons balsamic vinegar
> 1½ tablespoons Dijon mustard
> 1 heaping teaspoon snipped fresh dill, or ¼ teaspoon dried
> Salt and pepper
> 16 toothpicks

Soak plank according to instructions on page xix.

Wash and dry butter lettuce and tear into bite-size pieces. Set aside.

Tightly wrap a bacon slice around each shrimp, skewer with toothpick, and sprinkle with garlic salt.

Prepare plank for grilling according to instructions on page xx. Place shrimp on plank. Close lid and grill for 7 minutes, or until bacon is crisp.

To make the dressing, while shrimp is grilling emulsify olive oil, vinegar, mustard, dill, and salt and pepper. Place greens in a large salad bowl, add shrimp to greens, and coat well with vinaigrette. Portion salad onto 4 serving plates and top each plate with 4 shrimp. Remove toothpicks before serving.

MAKES 4 SERVINGS

Calamari Steaks *on* Mizuna

by: DINA GUILLEN

PLANK PREFERENCE: **ALL**

My dad used to work for an oil company based out of a Persian Gulf town in Saudi Arabia. My brother, sister, and I were born and raised there, and the Persian Gulf was our playground, as well as the source for wonderful seafood. While my mom watched over us as we were sailing or building sand castles on the beach, my dad would go fishing for some of the most exquisite-tasting fish in the world. The Persian Gulf is home to some of the best seafood I have ever tasted, and we would often end the day grilling dinner on the beach and then climbing the closest sand dune to stargaze for hours. Grilled calamari with a light lemon sauce is one of my favorite meals. Placing it over greens can make it a complete meal. The mizuna greens have a nice bite to them that works well with the mild-tasting calamari. If you are not a fan of mizuna, you can substitute other types of greens with a similar spiciness, such as arugula or watercress.

Juice of 1 large lemon plus 3 tablespoons fresh lemon juice
¼ cup plus 2 tablespoons extra-virgin olive oil
2 large garlic cloves, minced
2 teaspoons chopped fresh thyme
⅛ teaspoon freshly ground black pepper plus more to taste
Four 8- to 10-ounce calamari steaks
½ teaspoon salt
3 cups mizuna
2 ripe tomatoes, sliced
1 small red onion, thinly sliced

Soak plank according to instructions on page xix.

To make the marinade, mix the juice of 1 large lemon, ¼ cup olive oil, garlic, 1 teaspoon thyme, and ⅛ teaspoon pepper. Marinate calamari in sauce for 10 minutes at room temperature.

Prepare plank for grilling according to instructions on page xx. Place calamari steaks on plank. Close lid and grill for 6 minutes, or until calamari turns white and opaque. Do not overcook or the calamari will be rubbery. Remove from plank and allow to rest for 3 to 5 minutes. Slice steaks at an angle into thin strips.

To make the dressing, while calamari is grilling whisk together the remaining olive oil, remaining lemon juice, remaining thyme, and the salt in a medium bowl. Gently toss mizuna, tomatoes, and onion with dressing. Divide in 4 bowls and top with sliced calamari steaks. Add pepper to taste.

MAKES 4 SERVINGS

Lobster Tails *with* Orange Brandy Butter

by: MICHELLE LOWREY

PLANK PREFERENCE: **CEDAR**

The plank with all its smoky goodness does something magical to lobster. It takes me back to the grilled lobsters that I loved to devour whenever I was in Rosarita, Mexico. If you use frozen lobster tails, make sure they are completely thawed before starting this recipe. Try this dish the next time you have friends over for a barbecue. It is easy to prepare, and people will be impressed by your culinary prowess!

Four 8-ounce fresh or frozen lobster tails
2 tablespoons extra-virgin olive oil
Salt and pepper
2 tablespoons plus ½ cup unsalted butter
3 small garlic cloves, minced
¼ cup brandy
3 tablespoons orange juice
1 teaspoon lime zest
2 teaspoons coarse-grain mustard
2 tablespoons minced fresh tarragon, or 2 teaspoons dried
1 tablespoon chopped fresh basil, or 1 teaspoon dried

Soak plank according to instructions on page xix.

Butterfly the lobster tails by using kitchen shears or a sharp knife to cut lengthwise through the center of the top shell and meat. Cut to, but not through, bottom shell, being careful not to cut lobster tails in half. Spread tail open so meat is on top. Brush with olive oil and sprinkle liberally with salt and pepper. Set aside.

To make sauce, in a large saucepan melt 2 tablespoons butter over medium heat and add garlic, cooking until nicely browned. Add brandy, orange juice, lime zest, mustard, herbs, and remaining butter and combine well. Bring to a simmer and cook for 1 minute before taking pan off heat. Set aside.

Prepare plank for grilling according to instructions on page xx. Place lobster tails on plank, meat side up. Close lid and grill for 12 to 14 minutes, being careful not to overcook. Lobster is done when meat is opaque and flakes easily with a fork.

Cover lobster tails loosely with foil while butter sauce is reheated, if necessary. Place lobster tails on serving platter and drizzle with hot butter mixture. Serve immediately.

MAKES 4 SERVINGS

Sea Scallops Wrapped *in* Pancetta *with* Asparagus *and* Cherry Tomatoes

by: MARIA EVERLY

PLANK PREFERENCE: **ALL**

This is a very easy dish to prepare with wonderful results. The nutty taste of butter complements the sweetness of the scallops without compromising their delicate flavor, and the wood smoke works magic on the crispy pancetta. This dish can be served as a meal or as an elegant hors d'oeuvre. Use the freshest scallops available and be careful not to overcook. Substitute bay or calico scallops when sea scallops are not available.

> 16 medium sea scallops, about 1½ pounds
> 16 pancetta slices, or 8 bacon slices, halved
> 16 cherry tomatoes
> 4 asparagus spears, trimmed and cut into 1-inch pieces
> 2 tablespoons butter
> 2 teaspoons lemon juice
> ½ teaspoon garlic salt
> 1 large lemon, cut in half
> 4 bamboo skewers, soaked in water for 1 hour

Soak plank according to instructions on page xix.

Wrap each scallop with a pancetta slice. If needed, use a toothpick broken in half to hold pancetta.

In an alternating pattern on skewer, lace 4 scallops, 4 cherry tomatoes, and 4 pieces of asparagus. Place skewers in a large shallow baking dish and set aside.

Melt butter in a small saucepan on the stovetop, or microwave in a microwave-safe dish (about 30 seconds). Add lemon juice and garlic salt to butter and mix well. Pour butter mixture over the skewers, turning once.

Prepare plank for grilling according to instructions on page xx. Place skewers on plank. Close lid and grill for about 6 minutes or until the scallops are white and opaque. Do not overcook or scallops will become rubbery. Remove scallops from grill, squeeze lemon over scallops, and serve.

MAKES 4 APPETIZER SERVINGS

Clams *and* Mussels *with* Basil *and* Tomato Salsa

by: DINA GUILLEN

PLANK PREFERENCE: **CEDAR**

This dish is really good just as an appetizer, or if you prefer to make it as part of your entrée, serve it with Vegetable and Couscous Salad with Basil and Caper Vinaigrette (page 100). Pile the couscous salad in the center of your serving platter, and circle the couscous with the clams and mussels topped with salsa. It is very important to place the clams and mussels in a single layer on the plank so they absorb the flavor of the wood. If they do not all fit, grill them in two batches. Be careful not to overcook them because they dry out quickly.

2 plum tomatoes, finely diced
1 garlic clove, minced
1 teaspoon chopped fresh basil
1 large lemon, juiced
¼ cup extra-virgin olive oil
1 teaspoon salt
⅛ teaspoon freshly ground pepper
1 pound littleneck clams, scrubbed
1 pound mussels, scrubbed

Soak plank according to instructions on page xix.

To make salsa, combine the tomatoes, garlic, basil, lemon juice, olive oil, salt, and pepper in a small bowl. Allow to sit at room temperature for 1 hour to allow flavors to intensify.

Preheat plank for grilling according to instructions on page xx. Arrange clams and mussels in a single layer on the plank. Close lid and grill for about 8 minutes, or until shells open. Discard any clams or mussels that do not open.

Arrange clams and mussels on serving platter. Spoon salsa on top and serve.

MAKES 6 SERVINGS

Vegetables *and* Side Dishes

Corn *on the* Cob

Stuffed Portobello Mushroom Caps

Corn Guacamole

Vegetable *and* Couscous Salad *with* Basil *and*
   Caper Vinaigrette

Grape Leaves Stuffed *with* Herbed Goat Cheese

Creole Stuffed Eggplant

Shrimp *and* Couscous Stuffed Tomatoes Topped *with*
   Goat Cheese

Southwest Stuffed Bell Peppers

Stuffed Artichokes

Carrots *with a* Balsamic Glaze

Parmesan Herbed Potatoes

Lemon Zested Asparagus

Spicy Corn Chowder

Stuffed Tomatoes

A *main course* is only as good as the accompanying side dishes. With plank grilling, not only can you cook the main dish on the plank, you can also plank-grill the side dishes. The beauty of the grilling plank is that it enhances the flavors of almost every vegetable. And the grilling process caramelizes the vegetables, which brings out their sweetness. Pair that sweetness with the complementary flavors of smoke and wood and you have vegetable dishes that truly pamper the palate.

Vegetables grilled on the plank taste extraordinary, and using the plank eliminates the hassle of having to keep vegetables from falling through the grill grate. So chop up those vegetables, put them on the plank, and prepare the delicious *Vegetable and Couscous Salad with Basil and Caper Vinaigrette* (page 100). We love *Shrimp and Couscous Stuffed Tomatoes Topped with Goat Cheese* (page 105); *Lemon Zested Asparagus* (page 113) couldn't be tastier next to a grilled steak; and *Carrots with Balsamic Glaze* (page 111) caramelize beautifully on the plank.

Corn *on the* Cob

by: DINA GUILLEN

PLANK PREFERENCE: **CEDAR**

My parents love to travel. One summer when we were kids, they took my brother, sister, and me to Cairo, Egypt, where streets were flowing with carts selling grilled corn on the cob. You couldn't pass one of those carts without succumbing to the mouthwatering aroma of the smoky sweet corn tantalizing your taste buds. I think I ate more corn during that two-week vacation than I did the entire year. Like music, food has a way of bringing back all those nostalgic memories. The smell and taste of grilled corn is a great one for me. When I started thinking of ways to use the grilling plank, this was the first recipe I created. After testing this recipe on several types of woods, I definitely recommend that you stick with cedar on this one. The sweetness and spiciness of the cedar really complements the corn unlike any other wood.

¼ **cup extra-virgin olive oil**
¼ **cup balsamic vinegar**
½ **tablespoon Worcestershire sauce**
½ **teaspoon dried thyme**
½ **teaspoon cayenne**
1 **teaspoon garlic powder**
1 **teaspoon coarse salt**
¼ **teaspoon freshly ground black pepper**
6 **ears corn, husks and silk removed**

Soak plank according to instructions on page xix.

In a small bowl, whisk together olive oil, vinegar, and Worcestershire sauce. In another small bowl, combine the spices. Brush corn with oil mixture. Sprinkle spice mixture evenly over the corn. Set aside.

Prepare plank for grilling according to instructions on page xx. Place corn on the plank. Close lid and grill for 20 minutes.

MAKES 6 SERVINGS

Stuffed Portobello Mushroom Caps

by: **MICHELLE LOWREY**

PLANK PREFERENCE: **CEDAR**

Portobello *mushrooms have such a woodsy, meaty flavor, they just scream to be grilled on the plank. These can be served as a side dish or as a first course. If you are pressed for time, canned tomatoes can be substituted for fresh ones. For dinner parties, I like to cut these into quarters and serve them as appetizers. Simply place a toothpick in each one, and presto, you're a master chef!*

> 4 large portobello mushrooms
> ¼ cup extra-virgin olive oil
> 2 cups ricotta cheese
> 4 ounces freshly grated Parmesan cheese
> 1 tablespoon dried Italian seasoning
> 1 tablespoon plus 2 teaspoons chopped fresh basil
> 2 small garlic cloves, minced
> 2 large tomatoes, skinned, seeded, and diced (about 1 cup)
> Salt and pepper

Soak plank according to instructions on page xix.

Carefully remove stems and gills of mushrooms with a small spoon, and brush caps inside and out with olive oil.

To make the stuffing, in a small bowl combine ricotta, Parmesan, Italian seasoning, 1 tablespoon of the basil, and garlic. Fill mushroom caps with cheese mixture. Spoon tomatoes over mushroom caps and top with remaining basil. Sprinkle with salt and pepper.

Prepare plank for grilling according to instructions on page xx. Place mushrooms on plank. Close lid and grill for 8 to 10 minutes, or until cheese is bubbly and lightly browned.

MAKES 4 SERVINGS

Corn Guacamole

by: DINA GUILLEN

PLANK PREFERENCE: **CEDAR**

I made this for a dinner party one night, and the whole bowl was devoured before I even had a chance to get dinner on the table. This is a great recipe because it can be prepared ahead of time, allowing the smokiness from the grilled corn to infuse into the dip as it sits. The best type of avocado to use is the dark, thick-skinned Hass variety. Keeping the pits in the dip until serving helps prevent the guacamole from oxidizing.

2 ears corn, husks and silk removed
½ large red onion, cut into ¼-inch-thick slices
2 large ripe avocados
1 jalapeño, seeded and finely chopped
1½ tablespoons light mayonnaise
2 tablespoons extra-virgin olive oil
Juice of 1 large lime
¼ cup chopped fresh cilantro
1 teaspoon salt
¼ teaspoon freshly ground pepper
Corn chips

Soak plank according to instructions on page xix.

Prepare plank for grilling according to instructions on page xx. Place corn and red onion slices on plank. Close lid and grill for 15 minutes. Remove from heat and cool. When the corn is cool, cut the kernels off the cob and roughly chop the onion.

Peel avocados, remove the avocado pits, and reserve. Put avocados in a medium bowl and mash with a fork. Add corn, onion, jalapeño, mayonnaise, olive oil, lime juice, cilantro, salt, and pepper and mix well. Serve with corn chips. If not serving immediately, store the avocado pits in the center of the mixture, cover tightly, and refrigerate for up to 4 hours.

MAKES 6 SERVINGS

Vegetable *and* Couscous Salad *with* Basil *and* Caper Vinaigrette

by: DINA GUILLEN

PLANK PREFERENCE: **CEDAR**

I chose some of my favorite vegetables when creating this dish, but almost any seasonal vegetable can be substituted for those suggested here. For a full entrée, pair the couscous salad with Clams and Mussels with Basil and Tomato Salsa (page 94). Just pile the couscous salad in the center of a platter, and surround it with the clams and mussels. It makes a beautiful presentation for a dinner party.

¾ cup couscous
1 cup boiling water
1 small Japanese eggplant, peeled and cut into 1-inch cubes
4 asparagus spears, cut into 1-inch diagonal slices
1 large red pepper, cut into 1-inch diagonal slices
One 8½-ounce can quartered artichoke hearts, drained
½ cup cherry tomatoes, halved
1 medium red onion, peeled and quartered
½ cup whole mushrooms, quartered
⅓ cup plus 2 tablespoons extra-virgin olive oil
2 teaspoons coarse salt plus more to taste
½ teaspoon freshly ground black pepper plus more to taste
¼ cup fresh lemon juice
1 teaspoon Dijon mustard
1 tablespoon capers, drained
¼ cup chopped fresh basil

Soak plank according to instructions on page xix.

Combine couscous and boiling water in a medium bowl and let stand, covered, for 20 minutes. Fluff with a fork and cool slightly.

While couscous is standing, mix vegetables in a large bowl with 2 tablespoons of the olive oil, salt, and pepper.

Prepare plank for grilling according to instructions on page xx. Place vegetables on plank. Close lid and grill for 12 to 15 minutes. Remove from grill and set aside.

To make the vinaigrette, whisk together the lemon juice and mustard in a small bowl. Add remaining olive oil in a slow stream, whisking until emulsified. Stir in capers and basil.

Gently toss grilled vegetables with couscous and vinaigrette. Season with salt and pepper to taste.

MAKES 8 SERVINGS

Grape Leaves Stuffed *with* Herbed Goat Cheese

by: DINA GUILLEN

PLANK PREFERENCE: **MAPLE**

These delicious appetizers can be served simply on a platter garnished with rosemary sprigs or accompanied with grilled crusty bread, sliced ripe tomatoes, and chopped kalamata olives. They are perfect for a party since they can be prepared a day in advance and then grilled and served warm or at room temperature. If you are using fresh grape leaves, it is important to remove the stems and blanch the leaves in boiling water for 5 minutes before wrapping them around the goat cheese. It is best to prepare these rolls on a less assertive-tasting wood like maple because their flavor is so delicate.

1 tablespoon chopped fresh rosemary
1 tablespoon chopped fresh thyme
12 grape leaves, brined in jar, rinsed and stemmed
⅓ cup extra-virgin olive oil
One 11-ounce log goat cheese, cut into 12 pieces
Freshly ground black pepper

Soak plank according to instructions on page xix.

In a small bowl, combine rosemary and thyme. Fan grape leaves, vein side (dull side) up, on a work surface. Put the olive oil in a medium shallow dish, dip a cheese piece in oil, and place in center of 1 grape leaf. Sprinkle ¼ teaspoon of rosemary-thyme mixture over cheese and add a pinch of freshly ground pepper. Fold sides of leaves over cheese, fold up bottom, and continue to roll up. Repeat with remaining grape leaves. Place grape-leaf rolls back in dish with olive oil, cover, and chill for 1 hour or up to overnight.

Prepare plank for grilling according to instructions on page xx. Place grape-leaf rolls seam side down on plank. Close lid and grill for 6 minutes. The grape leaves will be soft and are meant to be eaten with the goat cheese.

MAKES 12 ROLLS

Creole Stuffed Eggplant

by: DINA GUILLEN

PLANK PREFERENCE: **CEDAR**

If you like stuffed eggplant, you need to try this version of it. Plank-grilling the stuffed eggplant on cedar infuses it with a sweetness and smokiness and turns this dish into an exhilarating entrée or side dish. This recipe calls for fresh bread crumbs. The easiest way to prepare them is by taking a few slices of day-old French or Italian bread, tearing them into chunks, and pulsing them in a food processor. There is no need to remove the crusts.

4 Japanese eggplants, or 2 medium eggplants
1 pound Italian sausage
3 tablespoons extra-virgin olive oil
1 medium red bell pepper, chopped
2 stalks celery, chopped
1 medium onion, chopped
1 tablespoon chopped garlic
1 cup chopped mushrooms
1 teaspoon dried thyme
½ teaspoon cayenne
½ teaspoon salt plus more for prepping the eggplant
¼ teaspoon pepper
1 cup fresh bread crumbs
1 cup Parmesan cheese, shredded
1 cup mozzarella cheese, shredded

Soak plank according to instructions on page xix.

Cut the eggplants in half lengthwise and, with a spoon, hollow out the center of each half to make a boatlike shell about ¼ inch thick. Sprinkle the interior shell with a few pinches of salt and set aside to drain. Finely chop the eggplant pulp and set aside.

To make the stuffing, in a large skillet brown sausage over medium-high heat. Remove browned sausage from skillet and set aside. Heat 2 tablespoons of the olive oil over medium-high heat in the same skillet. Sauté bell pepper, celery, onion, and garlic until soft, about 20 minutes. Add eggplant pulp and mushrooms to mixture and cook over medium heat until most of the water is evaporated. Add thyme, cayenne, salt, and pepper. Stir to combine and set aside to cool.

Pat dry eggplant shells. Lightly brush each shell with remaining oil. Turn vegetable mixture into a large bowl and fold in sausage, bread crumbs, and ½ cup of the Parmesan. Fill eggplant shells and set aside.

To make cheese topping, mix remaining Parmesan with mozzarella in a small bowl and set aside.

Prepare plank for grilling according to instructions on page xx. Place stuffed eggplant shells on plank. Close lid and grill for 20 to 25 minutes for Japanese eggplants, 35 to 40 minutes for medium eggplants. Open grill and sprinkle cheese topping evenly over each stuffed eggplant shell, close lid, and grill for an additional 3 minutes.

MAKES 8 SIDE DISHES OR 4 ENTRÉES

Shrimp *and* Couscous Stuffed Tomatoes Topped *with* Goat Cheese

by: DINA GUILLEN

PLANK PREFERENCE: **ALL**

I come from a family that loves to cook, and everyone is good at it, from my parents to my brother, sister, aunts, uncles, and cousins. You are guaranteed a great meal in any of their homes. One thing I have noticed about my family's cooking (and eating) habits is that we like to use fresh ingredients. My mom rarely opens a can, and I never tried a frozen TV dinner until I was well into my twenties and living on my own. We love our fresh vegetables any way they can be prepared, and if it can be stuffed, my mom will stuff it. Everything from cabbage, zucchini, peppers, eggplant—you name it. One of my favorite things to make is stuffed tomatoes. There are some foods that work particularly well with smoke- and wood-infused flavors, and tomatoes are one of them. The small, Moroccan-style couscous works best in this recipe.

4 large ripe tomatoes (2½ to 3 inches in diameter)
Salt
½ teaspoon mustard powder
¼ cup extra-virgin olive oil
1 tablespoon balsamic vinegar
1 shallot, minced
2 garlic cloves, minced
1 tablespoon chopped fresh basil
1 cup cooked salad shrimp, about ½ pound
1 cup cooked couscous, cooled
½ teaspoon salt
¼ teaspoon pepper
4 ounces crumbled goat cheese

Soak plank according to instructions on page xix.

Cut the tops off each tomato. Scoop out the pulp and discard. Sprinkle the interior shells of the tomatoes with a few pinches of salt and invert on paper towels to drain.

To make the stuffing, in a large bowl whisk together the mustard powder, olive oil, vinegar, shallot, garlic, and basil. Add the shrimp, couscous, salt, and pepper and stir to combine. Fill the tomato cavities with the couscous mixture.

Prepare plank for grilling according to instructions on page xx. Place stuffed tomatoes on plank. Close lid and grill for 10 to 15 minutes. Open grill and sprinkle crumbled goat cheese over each tomato, close lid, and grill for an additional 2 minutes. The tomatoes will soften as a result of grilling. Using a slotted spoon, carefully remove them from the plank and serve.

MAKES 4 SERVINGS

Southwest Stuffed Bell Peppers

by: DINA GUILLEN

PLANK PREFERENCE: **ALL**

This is one of those dishes I prefer plank grilled instead of the traditional method of baking. Plank grilling really showcases the smoky taste of fire-roasted bell peppers. You can use red or green bell peppers in this recipe—they both work wonderfully. Be sure to choose peppers that sit well on a flat surface. Also, if you have warmer racks on your grill, remember to remove them since they may knock over your bell peppers while the grill lid is being opened or closed.

4 large red or green bell peppers
3 tablespoons tomato paste
¾ cup beer
¾ cup ketchup
2 tablespoons extra-virgin olive oil
1 medium onion, chopped
3 garlic cloves, minced
1 pound ground beef
1 cup frozen corn kernels, thawed
1 cup cooked white rice
1½ teaspoons salt
½ teaspoon freshly ground black pepper
½ teaspoon ground cumin
½ teaspoon ancho chile powder
1 cup pepper Jack cheese, shredded

Soak plank according to instructions on page xix.

Cut tops off bell peppers and discard stems. Chop pepper tops to measure 1 cup. Remove and discard seeds and membranes from pepper bottoms and set aside.

Combine tomato paste and beer in a medium bowl, stirring well with a whisk. Add ketchup, mix well, and set aside.

Heat olive oil in a large skillet over medium heat. Add chopped pepper tops, onion, and garlic. Add the ground beef and sauté together until the beef is completely cooked. Drain fat. Add the corn and rice and cook for 1 minute. Add salt, pepper, cumin, chile powder, and half of the tomato sauce mixture. Stir well. Remove from heat and allow to cool slightly.

Spoon the stuffing into the prepared bell peppers and set aside.

Prepare plank for grilling according to instructions on page xx. Place stuffed bell peppers on plank and spoon remaining tomato sauce mixture over each bell pepper. Close lid and grill for 15 to 20 minutes. Open grill and sprinkle ¼ cup cheese over each bell pepper, close lid, and grill for an additional 2 minutes.

MAKES 4 SERVINGS

Stuffed Artichokes

by: DINA GUILLEN

PLANK PREFERENCE: **CEDAR**

I met one of my best friends, Jennifer Post, in high school. It was a new school for me, and it took a while to adjust and make new friends, but when I met Jenny I knew I had found a friend for life. Our school was located on the Monterey Peninsula in California, home to some of the best restaurants in the world. We quickly acquired an appreciation for good food. While I loved to experiment and try anything that was different, Jenny would inevitably order artichokes if they were on the menu. To this day, Jen is an artichoke aficionado, and I couldn't write a cookbook without creating a recipe dedicated to my artichoke-loving friend. The fresh herb stuffing in this recipe soaks in the scent of the smoke, while the artichoke is infused with the flavor of the wood. Make sure you use fresh bread crumbs for this dish.

4 large artichokes
½ cup fresh lemon juice, plus ½ large lemon
½ cup extra-virgin olive oil
3 cups fresh bread crumbs
2 large tomatoes, peeled, seeded, and diced
⅔ cup chopped fresh parsley
½ cup chopped fresh mint
2 tablespoons chopped fresh basil
6 garlic cloves, minced
6 green onions, chopped
1 teaspoon salt
¼ teaspoon pepper

Soak plank according to instructions on page xix.

Trim tops of artichoke leaves to remove pointed tips. Cut the stems straight across, leaving a level base so the artichokes will stand upright. Remove the tough outer leaves at the base. With a sharp knife, slice the tops of the artichokes straight across, taking off about 1 inch. Rub the lemon on the cut ends to prevent oxidation.

Place the artichokes in a large pot with salted water. Squeeze the juice of the lemon into the water, adding the squeezed lemon half. Bring to a boil over high heat, then reduce to a simmer and cook for 30 to 35 minutes, or until the artichokes are barely tender. Drain and cool.

While the artichokes are cooking, prepare the stuffing. In a large bowl, combine the lemon juice with all remaining ingredients and mix well. Spread the artichoke leaves apart and fill the spaces between the leaves with the stuffing mixture.

Prepare plank for grilling according to instructions on page xx. Place stuffed artichokes on plank. Close lid and grill for 15 to 20 minutes, or until leaves come off easily.

MAKES 4 SERVINGS

Carrots *with a* **Balsamic Glaze**

by: MICHELLE LOWREY

PLANK PREFERENCE: **CEDAR**

Growing up in Colorado, the winter season would drag on forever, while the summer seemed to be gone before you knew it. Both my parents loved to garden and, because of the short growing season, they would be out in the garden fast and furious come the last frost in May. We had a huge garden with rows and rows of corn, watermelon, squash, zucchini that could not be tamed, and, of course, carrots. As a child I loved to go through the garden rows inspecting how things were growing. I loved the tender carrot tops as they just sprouted through the soil, so delicate and soft. In the summer, I probably ate carrots every day. Today, my kids are not the fan of vegetables that I once was, but every time I make these carrots I know they will not only eat them, but love them.

4 large carrots, peeled and halved lengthwise
2 tablespoons soy sauce
2 tablespoons honey
1 tablespoon balsamic vinegar
1½ tablespoons extra-virgin olive oil
3 large garlic cloves, minced
1 tablespoon chopped fresh parsley

Soak plank according to instructions on page xix.

Parboil carrots in a large pot of boiling water over medium-high heat for 5 minutes. Rinse with cold water and drain. Place carrots in a large glass baking dish.

Combine remaining ingredients except for parsley together in a small bowl and pour mixture over carrots, combining well. Marinate carrots for 1 hour at room temperature.

Prepare plank for grilling according to instructions on page xx. Place carrot halves on plank. Close lid and grill for 10 minutes. Carrots will be caramelized and slightly charred. Top with chopped parsley just before serving.

MAKES 4 SERVINGS

Parmesan Herbed Potatoes

by: **MICHELLE LOWREY**

PLANK PREFERENCE: **CEDAR**

Potatoes on the plank are easy to make and are a versatile side dish. I especially love the Parmesan cheese crust that forms on the potatoes after they are done cooking. The smoky flavor of these potatoes adds an interesting dimension that would pair well with beef, chicken, or fish.

> 2 large baking potatoes, halved
> ¼ cup freshly grated Parmesan cheese
> 2 tablespoons extra-virgin olive oil
> 1 tablespoon chopped fresh parsley, or 1 teaspoon dried
> 3 large garlic cloves, minced
> ½ teaspoon salt
> ¼ teaspoon pepper
> ¼ teaspoon dried Italian seasoning
> Sour cream (optional)

Soak plank according to instructions on page xix.

Parboil potatoes in a large pot of boiling salted water over medium-high heat until tender but firm, about 15 minutes. Drain potatoes, pat dry, and allow them to cool.

In a large bowl, combine all remaining ingredients except sour cream. Cut potatoes into ¼-inch slices and coat well with Parmesan mixture.

Prepare plank for grilling according to instructions on page xx. Place potato slices on plank. Close lid and grill for 15 minutes. To serve, top potatoes with a dollop of sour cream, if desired.

MAKES 4 SERVINGS

Lemon Zested Asparagus

by: MICHELLE LOWREY

PLANK PREFERENCE: **CEDAR**

I*t may have been those hearty main course dishes like pork, chicken, and fish that got us interested in plank grilling, but for me, the vegetables are what kept me going back to experiment night after night. Vegetables are easy to make and taste great when plank grilled. I love the smoky sweetness that is created, and I know that just a few minutes after the grill is hot I will have a wonderful vegetable dish ready to put on the table. Asparagus is a great vegetable to plank-grill because it soaks up the smoky flavor quickly, and I do not have to worry about the delicate spears falling through the grate.*

    ¼ **cup extra-virgin olive oil**
    2 tablespoons fresh lemon juice
    1 tablespoon chopped fresh dill, or 1 teaspoon dried
    ½ **teaspoon kosher salt**
    2 large garlic cloves, minced
    1 pound fresh asparagus, washed with bottom woody stems removed
    Zest of 1 small lemon

Soak plank according to instructions on page xix.

Combine the olive oil, lemon juice, dill, salt, and garlic in a large glass baking dish. Add asparagus and marinate at room temperature for 1 hour.

Prepare plank for grilling according to instructions on page xx. Place asparagus spears on plank. Close lid and grill for 5 to 7 minutes, until spears are tender but firm. Top with lemon zest before serving.

MAKES 6 SERVINGS

Spicy Corn Chowder

by: **MICHELLE LOWREY** *and* **DINA GUILLEN**

PLANK PREFERENCE: **CEDAR**

Michelle grew up in Colorado where, because of its proximity to New Mexico, she ate many foods inspired by Southwestern flavors. She loved visiting Santa Fe, where she could not get enough of the amazing Indian fry bread or blue corn tortillas. A couple of years ago, she got the opportunity to take her husband, Corey, to New Mexico to show him the state that she loved so much. "As we seem to do whenever we go on vacation," she said, "we ate our way through that beautiful state." This soup was inspired by a corn soup that they both loved in Santa Fe. Use the amazing Corn on the Cob to make this chowder. The cedar plank imparts such a rustic and wonderful flavor to corn, and the adobo sauce from the chipotle pepper makes this soup a vibrant pink color that is so pretty.

> 6 ears Corn on the Cob (page 97)
> 2 cups low-sodium chicken broth
> 1 large chipotle pepper, diced (from a jar of chipotle peppers in
>   adobo sauce)
> 4 small garlic cloves, chopped
> 4 cups heavy whipping cream
> 2 tablespoons white wine vinegar
> ¼ teaspoon salt
> ¼ teaspoon pepper

With a sharp knife, cut kernels off corn cobs to measure 4 cups. Set half the corn kernels aside.

In a food processor, combine the other half of the corn with the chicken broth, chipotle, and garlic and pulse until creamy and smooth. If corn mixture is too thick, add water a tablespoon at a time.

Transfer mixture to a large pot and add reserved corn, whipping cream, vinegar, salt, and pepper. Stirring occasionally, bring mixture to a boil over medium heat until slightly thickened, about 5 minutes.

MAKES 6 SERVINGS

Stuffed Tomatoes

by: GRETCHEN BERNSDORFF

PLANK PREFERENCE: **MAPLE**

The "what to have with it" and "is it nutritious" decisions are my two main challenges in menu planning. A unique and effective approach is to let color guide the selections. A meal with a balanced color palette is frequently nutritionally balanced as well. Find a food that matches the missing color and the two main challenges are resolved. Finding the missing color is almost like decorating a room. Start with a color that inspires you. I love a big, bold red (the secret to the rich, red color typically associated with tomatoes is lycopene, which has been found to fight heart disease and cancer). To continue decorating my plate, I just think about what colors go well with reds. Vibrant greens and earthy browns are safe bets that blend nicely with reds. It is then easy to see that stuffing tomatoes with ground turkey and serving them alongside a spinach salad creates a meal balanced in color and nutrition.

6 large vine-ripened tomatoes
1 tablespoon butter
½ pound ground turkey
2 tablespoons granulated garlic
Salt and pepper
1 cup fresh bread crumbs
1 egg, beaten
2 tablespoons extra-virgin olive oil
2 shallots, finely diced
1 tablespoon Dijon mustard
½ cup freshly grated Parmesan cheese

Soak plank according to instructions on page xix.

Cut the tops off the tomatoes. Scoop out the pulp and discard. Set tomatoes aside.

In a small skillet, melt the butter over medium-high heat. Add the turkey and garlic and cook until turkey is browned. Season with salt and pepper to taste.

In a large bowl, combine the turkey mixture with the remaining ingredients. Spoon the mixture evenly into the tomatoes.

Prepare plank for grilling according to instructions on page xx. Place stuffed tomatoes on plank. Close lid and grill for 15 minutes. The tomatoes will soften as a result of grilling. Using a slotted spoon, carefully remove them from the plank and serve.

MAKES 6 SERVINGS

Breads *and* Desserts

California Pizza

Chicken, Artichoke, *and* Sun-Dried Tomato Panini

Beer Bread

Vegetable *and* Gouda Quesadillas

Strawberries *with* Lemon Cream Parfait

Peaches *with* Crème Fraîche Topping

Pound Cake *with* Chocolate Amaretto Sauce

Pecan *and* Cinnamon Stuffed Apples *with* Caramel Sauce

Peach Sorbet

Pineapple Sundaes

Crepes Stuffed *with* Peaches *and* Topped *with*
    Cinnamon Caramel Sauce

Dessert is that end-of-the-meal signature that puts an exclamation point on any dinner. A bad main course can be saved by a great dessert. Serve someone a killer chocolate sundae, for example, and all is forgotten. On the other hand, a great main course can be slightly tarnished when the last bite of a meal is a bland dessert. The recipes included here are highly original and far from bland.

While it may seem unusual to use a grilling plank to cook desserts and bread, it seemed like a great transition to us because of how well the plank keeps an even, constant heat. The smokiness that permeates *Chicken, Artichoke, and Sun-Dried Tomato Panini* (page 121) and the crust of *Beer Bread* (page 123) will make you a believer that bread cooked with smoke is a sublime experience. Cooking *California Pizza* (page 119) on the plank is so easy and delicious, you will soon be experimenting with your own favorite sauces and toppings. We recommend keeping extra pizza dough handy for those days when only homemade pizza will do. Breads cooked on a plank remind us of food cooked in a wood-burning oven, only you do not need to heat your house past the boiling point on a hot summer day.

Leave it to women to come up with a recipe using chocolate for the grill. *Pound Cake with Chocolate Amaretto Sauce* (page 130) is a show stopper. The crispy coconut shell is reminiscent of a s'more as you bite through the smoky and creamy pound cake that finishes with a gooey chocolate sauce.

A slight smoky taste in fruit lends a sophisticated air to your food that is quite enjoyable and surprisingly delectable. *Peaches with Crème Fraîche Topping* (page 129) and *Strawberries with Lemon Cream Parfait* (page 127) are two examples of how the grilling plank can make dessert on the patio something to remember. You certainly will remember *Peach Sorbet* (page 133), because grilling brings out the sweetness of the peaches and makes a gorgeous dessert. Desserts made on the grill are always easy and quick to prepare, so you know that in no time flat you will have something sweet that is unique and delicious.

California Pizza

by: GRETCHEN BERNSDORFF

PLANK PREFERENCE: **ALDER** *or* **OAK**

At first it seemed unusual to grill a pizza, but then I realized that plank-grilling pizza emulates the traditional wood-fired taste you get in a restaurant. Plank grilling is much more cost effective than remodeling your kitchen to include a wood-burning oven. Depending on the occasion, this pizza dresses up as gourmet pizza for entertaining friends. It is playful enough to please the kids and special enough to just savor by yourself. This recipe makes one plank-size pizza, but it can easily be doubled. You can also vary the topping amounts depending on how much you want on your pizza—load it up or keep it light. Dusting the plank with cornmeal is essential to ensure the dough does not stick to the wood.

½ package active dry yeast (1⅛ teaspoons)
¾ cup water at 105 degrees F
¾ cup all-purpose flour
1 cup whole-wheat flour
1 tablespoon extra-virgin olive oil
½ teaspoon salt
½ tablespoon honey
2 garlic cloves, minced
¼ teaspoon dried basil
¼ teaspoon dried oregano
One 14½-ounce can Italian stewed tomatoes, diced
One 12-ounce can tomato paste
⅛ teaspoon dried Italian seasoning
1 bay leaf
½ tablespoon chicken bouillon granules, dissolved in 3 tablespoons
    water
½ teaspoon sugar
2 tablespoons balsamic vinegar
Freshly ground pepper
1 tomato, sliced
¼ cup chopped olives
½ cup chopped artichoke hearts

½ small red onion, diced
½ cup thinly sliced mushrooms
½ cup sun-dried tomatoes
1½ cups shredded mozzarella cheese
Cooking spray
2 tablespoons cornmeal for dusting plank

Soak plank according to instructions on page xix.

To make the dough, combine the yeast and water and let proof for 5 minutes. Add the flours, olive oil, salt, honey, garlic, basil, and oregano and knead for about 10 minutes. Coat the dough and a clean bowl with cooking spray. Put the dough in the bowl, cover with plastic wrap, and let rise until doubled in size, about 1½ hours.

While the dough is rising, make the sauce. In a small saucepan, combine the tomatoes, tomato paste, Italian seasoning, bay leaf, bouillon, sugar, and vinegar. Add freshly ground pepper to taste. Bring to a boil, then reduce heat and simmer for 1½ hours. If the sauce becomes too thick, add a splash of water.

When the dough has risen, remove it from the bowl. Punch the dough down and reshape it into a log shape. Re-cover the dough with plastic wrap and allow to rest for 10 minutes.

Prepare plank for grilling according to instructions on page xx. Lightly spray one side with cooking spray and dust with cornmeal.

On a floured work surface, flatten the dough into a rectangle slightly larger than the plank. Place the dough on plank (it should hang off the edges). Fold up and pinch the edges to the size of the plank.

Spread the sauce on the dough. Add toppings, finishing with the cheese. Close lid and grill for 15 minutes, or until the crust browns and the cheese is slightly starting to brown.

MAKES 4 SERVINGS

Chicken, Artichoke, *and* Sun–Dried Tomato Panini

by: GRETCHEN BERNSDORFF

PLANK PREFERENCE: **ALDER**

Truly, I think I could live off peanut butter sandwiches, but sometimes I want a little more sophistication in my food. And I think it is a sin to live in California and not take advantage of the local flavors. I had never seen an artichoke crop until I moved to the West Coast, so I certainly had no idea what to do with an artichoke. To figure it out, I bought a huge Costco-size jar of artichoke hearts and just started creating. The end result was a panini that eats like a meal and keeps me fueled until the next feeding time. The marinated, jarred artichokes add a lot of "California" to the traditional chicken sandwich. Additionally, the butter mixture can be used in your favorite chicken Kiev recipe, as a spread on bagels and breads, or melted on baked potatoes.

4 large chicken tenderloins, about 1 pound
2½ cups oil-and-vinegar salad dressing (I prefer Newman's Own)
One 6½-ounce jar marinated artichoke hearts, diced, with liquid
   reserved
Half a 10-ounce jar of sun-dried tomatoes in oil, diced
8 mushrooms, sliced
1 small red onion, sliced
2 tablespoons butter, softened
1 teaspoon minced garlic
1 tablespoon freshly grated Parmesan cheese
1 tablespoon chopped fresh parsley, or 1 teaspoon dried
8 slices fresh Pugliese bread, or any rustic, crusty bread
4 slices Monterey Jack cheese
1 cup fresh baby spinach leaves

Soak plank according to instructions on page xix.

Put chicken and 2 cups of the salad dressing in a large shallow glass pan, making sure dressing completely covers meat. Cover and marinate overnight.

Heat a large sauté pan over medium heat. Add artichokes, reserved artichoke liquid, sun-dried tomatoes, mushrooms, and onion. Sauté for about 5 minutes. Set aside.

To make the butter mixture, combine the butter, garlic, Parmesan, and parsley in a small bowl. Spread the mixture on both sides of all the bread slices. Set aside.

Prepare plank for grilling according to instructions on page xx. Place chicken on plank. Pour the remaining salad dressing over the chicken. Close lid and grill for 20 minutes, or until juices run clear. Remove chicken from grill and allow to rest for 5 minutes. Slice the chicken lengthwise and set aside.

Flip the plank over and place directly over low flame. Place the bread on the plank and grill for 5 minutes to melt the butter. Remove plank from grill and transfer bread slices directly onto grill. Add cheese slices to 4 pieces of bread, allowing the cheese to melt and the bread to brown. Remove all from grill.

Assemble sandwiches by layering the spinach, vegetables, and chicken on the slice of bread with cheese, and top with a plain slice. Cut in half and enjoy!

MAKES 4 PANINI

Beer Bread

by: GRETCHEN BERNSDORFF

PLANK PREFERENCE: **ALDER**

My father immigrated as a child to America from Austria. Our family is spread across Germany, Russia, and the United States. Family reunions are a blend of languages, lifestyles, dancing, singing, food, and drink. I can always count on having fresh *brot* (German for bread) and good beer. Rich in history, beer bread is interesting because the yeast in the beer promotes the leavening process. This particular recipe adds brown rice to create a unique texture. It is also possible to play with the types of flour used, and the recipe can easily be adjusted to make rye or pumpernickel bread. Baking bread on a plank is tricky at first. The temperature is crucial to getting a bread that is properly smoked, crunchy on the outside, and chewy on the inside. Be sure the plank is not too close to the heat source and that it has been properly soaked. The plank should only smolder and not catch fire. The inside of the bread will not bake if the grill lid is opened and closed too often. This recipe takes time, but gives me that soul-satisfying luxury of indulging in a mouthwatering, hearty, crusty bite of homemade bread that is reminiscent of family gatherings.

2 cups all-purpose flour, plus more for kneading
2 cups gluten flour, or bread flour
¾ cup cooked instant brown rice
¼ cup brown sugar
One packet active dry yeast (2¼ teaspoons)
1½ teaspoons salt
1¼ cups beer, room temperature
3 tablespoons heavy whipping cream, room temperature
Cooking spray
Cornmeal for dusting plank
Melted butter for brushing loaf
Kosher salt (optional)

Soak plank according to instructions on page xix.

Using a stand mixer or by hand, whisk together the flours, rice, brown sugar, yeast, and salt. Whisking the dry ingredients helps incorporate them evenly and simulates sifting the flours. Add beer and whipping cream. Using a dough hook, mix on low speed until dough forms. If a dough hook is unavailable, mix with a spoon, or even your hands, until dough forms into a ball.

Remove dough from mixer and knead by hand on a floured surface for 2 minutes. After kneading, form dough into a ball. It will be slightly larger than a softball at this point. Place dough in an oiled bowl, cover with plastic wrap, and put it in a warm place. Allow to rise a second time until doubled in size, approximately 30 minutes.

After the first rise, remove dough from bowl and punch down. Knead on a floured surface for about 1 minute. Do not overknead. Form dough into a loaf shape. Place loaf on an oiled cookie sheet, cover with plastic wrap, and allow to rise a second time until doubled in size.

Prepare plank for grilling according to instructions on page xx. Coat one side lightly with cooking spray and then dust it with cornmeal. Place the loaf on the plank. Lightly brush loaf with melted butter. Close lid and grill for about 40 minutes. Lightly brush loaf with butter after 15 minutes and again after 30 minutes. Remove loaf from plank immediately. Sprinkle with salt if desired.

MAKES 1 LOAF

Vegetable *and* Gouda Quesadillas

by: DINA GUILLEN *and* GRETCHEN BERNSDORFF

PLANK PREFERENCE: **CEDAR**

Y*ou know those moments when the most obvious idea evades you until some-one just happens to mention it out of the blue and you wonder why you didn't think of it in the first place? That's how this recipe came about. We were trying to think of dishes that would work particularly well plank-grilled. A friend was talking about how she had just seen Emeril on the Food Network prepare this really delicious quesa-dilla, and honestly, I can't remember another word she said after that. All I remember is the word "quesadilla," and I ran home to plank-grill some for dinner with a vegetable stuffing that Gretchen had created days earlier. This delicious grilled quesadilla has a smooth smoky taste. If you don't have Gouda, try making these quesadillas with any soft cheese like Fontina, Monterey Jack, or pepper Jack cheese.*

1 large red bell pepper, seeded and halved
1 large yellow bell pepper, seeded and halved
2 portobello mushroom caps
½ small butternut squash, peeled, seeded, and cut into
   ¼-inch thick slices
12 green onions
½ cup extra-virgin olive oil
4 teaspoons garlic salt
4 teaspoons dried marjoram
1 cup shredded Gouda cheese
16 corn tortillas
Sour cream

Soak plank according to instructions on page xix.

Put bell peppers, mushrooms, squash, and green onions in a large resealable plastic bag. Add the oil, garlic salt, and marjoram. Seal bag and gently shake to completely coat vegetables.

Prepare plank for grilling according to instructions on page xx. Remove vegetables from bag and place on prepared plank. Close lid and grill for 15 to 20 minutes, or until all vegetables are tender.

Remove vegetables from plank. Slice the peppers, mushrooms, and squash into thin strips. Dice the onions.

Place 2 tablespoons shredded cheese on a corn tortilla. Layer vegetables over cheese, and top with another corn tortilla. Repeat with remaining tortillas, cheese, and vegetables. Place quesadillas on plank, two at a time, and grill for 5 minutes. Serve with a dollop of sour cream.

MAKES 8 QUESADILLAS

Strawberries *with* Lemon Cream Parfait

by: MICHELLE LOWREY

PLANK PREFERENCE: CEDAR

This dish was inspired by me getting a little overzealous and buying a couple of flats of strawberries one afternoon. The cedar plank adds a wonderfully complex and robust flavor with an intensified sweetness to the strawberries. The lemon cream complements the berries perfectly and makes a beautiful presentation. This will wow your dinner guests or family alike, and if you have never tried strawberries on the plank before, this is just the recipe to make you a convert.

  1 quart strawberries, washed and hulled
  3 tablespoons unsalted butter, melted
  1 tablespoon vanilla extract
  1 tablespoon sugar
  ½ teaspoon cinnamon
  2 cups heavy whipping cream
  6 tablespoons superfine sugar
  ¼ cup sour cream
  2 tablespoons fresh lemon juice
  Zest of 1 small lemon

Soak plank according to instructions on page xix.

To make the strawberries, put berries in medium bowl and coat with melted butter and vanilla extract. Mix berries evenly with sugar and cinnamon.

Prepare plank for grilling according to instructions on page xx. Place strawberries directly on plank. Close lid and grill for 3 minutes. Turn strawberries over and continue grilling for 2 to 3 minutes, for a total cooking time of 5 to 6 minutes. Strawberries should be nicely caramelized. Remove from grill and allow to cool slightly. Put aside 6 whole strawberries for garnish, and chop the remaining berries roughly and put in a bowl. Cover and refrigerate until ready to assemble.

To make the lemon cream, combine the whipping cream and sugar and beat with an electric mixer on medium speed until soft peaks form. Add the sour cream, lemon juice, and lemon zest and beat until stiff but not dry peaks form. Keep covered in refrigerator until ready to assemble.

To assemble: Place a small amount of berries in the bottom of a parfait or wine glass and top with a dollop of lemon cream. Alternate layers of strawberries and lemon cream, finishing with a top layer of lemon cream. Repeat with the remaining strawberries and lemon cream. Garnish with reserved whole strawberries and serve.

MAKES 6 SERVINGS

Peaches *with* Crème Fraîche Topping

by: MICHELLE LOWREY

PLANK PREFERENCE: **CEDAR**

I worked as a pastry chef for several years before I decided to become a full-time stay-at-home mom to my two great kids. With my background in pastry, it seemed only natural to think of dessert recipes. This is the first recipe I created on the plank and one that I return to again and again. This is such a beautiful, sophisticated dessert.

5 tablespoons honey
2 tablespoons brandy
Juice of 1 small orange (about ¼ cup)
1 tablespoon lemon juice
¼ teaspoon cinnamon
¼ teaspoon nutmeg
8 ripe but firm peaches, skinned, halved, and pitted
1 cup crème fraîche
¼ cup sliced almonds, toasted

Soak plank according to instructions on page xix.

To make the marinade, combine 2 tablespoons of the honey, brandy, orange juice, lemon juice, and spices and pour into a large shallow glass baking dish. Place the peaches cut side down in baking dish, cover, and marinate for at least 30 minutes. Peaches can be marinated a few hours ahead.

Prepare plank for grilling according to instructions on page xx. Place the peaches cut side up on plank. Close lid and grill over low heat for 14 to 16 minutes, or until peaches are hot and the tops are caramelized.

While the peaches are grilling, mix the crème fraîche and 2 tablespoons of the honey in a small bowl.

To serve, place a dollop of crème fraîche in the center of each peach half. Place 2 peach halves on each plate and garnish with toasted almonds and the remaining honey.

MAKES 8 SERVINGS

Pound Cake *with* Chocolate Amaretto Sauce

by: MICHELLE LOWREY

PLANK PREFERENCE: **CEDAR**

This easy recipe reminds me of the s'mores I loved as a kid. Oh, who am I kid-ding? I still love them! Yet another reason I love to use the grilling plank for this cake is because it is a perfect way to help the cake slices cook evenly and stay in place on the grill. There will be plenty of chocolate sauce left over, so store the remainder for future use. If you do not like amaretto, substitute the liqueur or flavored extract of your choice.

1½ cups heavy whipping cream
12 ounces semisweet chocolate, finely chopped (1½ cups)
1 tablespoon amaretto liqueur
One 12-ounce store-bought pound cake
One 14-ounce can sweetened condensed milk
1 tablespoon almond extract
3 cups unsweetened flaked coconut

Soak plank according to instructions on page xix.

To make the chocolate amaretto sauce, in a small heavy-bottomed saucepan over medium heat bring cream just to a boil. Remove from heat and add chopped chocolate. Stir until smooth and chocolate has completely melted; add amaretto. Sauce can be prepared ahead of time, stored in an airtight container, and reheated over low heat just before serving.

Cut cake into 6 slices, 2 inches thick, and put in a large glass baking dish. With a fork, poke holes all over the slices so they can become as saturated as possible with the condensed milk mixture. In a small bowl, combine condensed milk and almond extract and pour over cake slices. Allow slices to sit for about 15 minutes.

Put coconut in a shallow dish and coat both sides of each cake slice with coconut.

Prepare plank for grilling according to instructions on page xx. Place cake slices on plank. Close lid and grill for 4 minutes. Carefully turn cake slices over, close lid, and grill another 2 to 3 minutes. Coconut should be very brown and nicely crisp.

To serve, spoon warm chocolate sauce onto a plate, cut one slice of cake in half on the diagonal and place halves decoratively on the sauce. Drizzle more sauce over the cake. Repeat for each slice and serve immediately.

MAKES 6 SERVINGS

Pecan *and* Cinnamon Stuffed Apples
with Caramel Sauce

by: DINA GUILLEN

PLANK PREFERENCE: **CEDAR**

This theory is by no means scientific, but I believe the world is made up of two kinds of people—those who prefer chocolate and those who prefer caramel. And, of course, there are people like my son who prefer sugar in any form, period. Personally, I am a caramel person. And since apples and caramel are one of my favorite combinations, I wanted to create a dessert that incorporated those two ingredients. The apples take really well to being grilled, and the cedar imparts an intensely complementary flavor that is not matched by any other wood. I always have a jar of caramel sauce in the pantry, and with the help of a prepared sauce this dessert is a snap to make.

    4 Rome or other baking apples, halved
    ½ cup pecans, finely chopped
    ¼ cup sugar
    ¼ teaspoon cinnamon
    ⅛ teaspoon nutmeg
    1 tablespoon melted butter
    Store-bought caramel sauce, heated

Soak plank according to instructions on page xix.

To prepare the apples, hollow out each apple half with a melon baller, removing the core and seeds and about 1 tablespoon of the flesh. Cut a small slice from the bottom of each apple half so it can lie flat on the plank.

To make the filling, combine the pecans, sugar, cinnamon, nutmeg, and melted butter in a small bowl, stirring until well combined. Spoon stuffing into each apple half and set aside.

Prepare plank for grilling according to instructions on page xx. Place stuffed apples on plank. Close lid and grill for 20 minutes, until apples are soft. Remove from grill, drizzle heated caramel sauce over each apple half, and serve.

MAKES 8 SERVINGS

Peach Sorbet

by: DINA GUILLEN

PLANK PREFERENCE: **MAPLE**

The first time I tried this recipe, I grilled the peaches on a cedar plank. The peaches tasted amazingly delicious on their own after they were grilled. In fact, they were great in a crepe (see Crepes Stuffed with Peaches and Topped with Cinnamon Caramel Sauce, page 136) or alongside some vanilla ice cream. However, after they were puréed and made into sorbet, the taste of the cedar overpowered the peaches. I tried it again on a maple plank, and what a difference. The peaches had a subtle smoky taste—just wonderful!

> 1 cup sugar
> 1 cup water
> 2 tablespoons lemon juice
> 4 large peaches (about 2 pounds), halved and pitted

Soak plank according to instructions on page xix.

Make a simple syrup by mixing the sugar and water in a medium saucepan and bringing to a boil over medium heat. Cook for 2 minutes. Remove from heat, add lemon juice, and allow to cool completely at room temperature. The simple syrup can be made in advance and refrigerated until you are ready to make the sorbet.

Prepare plank for grilling according to instructions on page xx. Place peach halves cut side down on plank. Close lid and grill for 20 minutes. Remove from plank and set aside until cool. Remove skins from peaches.

Purée peaches in a blender until smooth. Force purée through a sieve into a medium bowl. Discard any remaining pulp in sieve. Add the simple syrup to purée and whisk until combined. Pour mixture into an ice-cream maker and freeze according to manufacturer's directions.

MAKES 6 SERVINGS

Pineapple Sundaes

by: MICHELLE LOWREY

PLANK PREFERENCE: **CEDAR**

I love to cook with pineapple because of its versatility. Savory dishes such as chicken kebabs just would not be the same without that wedge of pineapple, and a Hawaiian pizza is unthinkable without it. This is a sophisticated twist on the ice-cream sundaes with the store-bought pineapple sauce you probably had as a kid. The pineapple is not overly sweet, and when served hot right off the grill over ice cream, they are such a treat. This recipe can make more or less than six servings, depending on the amount of fruit offered with each sundae.

1 cup light brown sugar
½ cup unsalted butter
2 tablespoons lemon juice
½ cup dark rum
2 tablespoons orange juice
1 teaspoon cinnamon
⅛ teaspoon ground cloves
1 large fresh pineapple (about 2 cups), peeled, cored, and cut into
    1-inch slices
Good-quality vanilla ice cream

Soak plank according to instructions on page xix.

To make sauce, in a large heavy-bottomed saucepan combine brown sugar, butter, lemon juice, rum, orange juice, and spices and bring to a boil over medium-high heat. Reduce heat to medium-low and simmer for 8 minutes, or until slightly thickened. Allow sauce to cool slightly.

134   *The* **Plank Grilling Cookbook**

Prepare plank for grilling according to instructions on page xx. Place pineapple slices on plank and baste liberally with sauce. Close lid and grill for 3 minutes. Turn pineapple slices, baste with sauce, close lid, and grill for another 2 to 3 minutes, or until pineapple is nicely caramelized and golden. Set remaining sauce aside for pouring over sundaes.

To serve, place 2 scoops of vanilla ice cream into serving bowl and top with fruit slices. Drizzle with desired amount of extra sauce and serve.

MAKES 6 SERVINGS

Crepes Stuffed *with* Peaches *and* Topped *with* Cinnamon Caramel Sauce

by: DINA GUILLEN, GRETCHEN BERNSDORFF, *and* MICHELLE LOWREY

PLANK PREFERENCE: **CEDAR**

We have learned that a big part of writing a cookbook is testing the recipes. We were going round and round during the testing process, deciding which recipes were good enough to include. There were three recipes with elements that were working spectacularly, which we just couldn't ignore, while other parts of those same recipes just kept failing, and we couldn't ignore that either. At one point, we decided to combine the crepes from one recipe, the grilled peaches from another, and the cinnamon caramel sauce from a third. We knew we had a winner. Fruit is so delicious grilled on cedar planks, especially strawberries, peaches, nectarines, apricots, and apples. You can make this recipe with any of those fruits. If you don't feel like making crepes, you can serve the plank-grilled fruit with a side of vanilla ice cream.

½ cup gluten flour
½ cup all-purpose flour
1 cup buttermilk
¾ cup lukewarm water
2 large eggs
1 egg white
2 tablespoons butter, melted
1 cup light brown sugar
½ cup unsalted butter
2 tablespoons lemon juice
¼ cup dark rum
2 tablespoons orange juice
1 teaspoon cinnamon
⅛ teaspoon ground cloves
4 large peaches (about 2 pounds), halved and pitted

Soak plank according to instructions on page xix.

Blend the flours, buttermilk, water, eggs, egg white, and melted butter in a blender or food processor and put in the refrigerator, and allow to rest for about 1 hour prior to use.

To make the sauce, in a large saucepan combine the brown sugar, butter, lemon juice, rum, orange juice, and spices and bring to a boil over medium-high heat. Reduce heat to medium-low and simmer for 5 minutes, or until slightly thickened. Allow sauce to cool slightly.

To make the crepes, remove the batter from the refrigerator and give it a quick stir. Put 3 tablespoons of batter in a seasoned crepe pan (or nonstick pan). Cook on one side until bubbles start to form and pop. Flip crepe and cook until lightly browned. Remove from pan. Crepes can be placed in a warm oven between sheets of wax paper until ready to use.

Prepare plank for grilling according to instructions on page xx. Place peach halves cut side down on plank. Close lid and grill for 14 to 16 minutes. Remove peaches from plank, carefully remove peach skins, and slice peaches.

To serve, fill each crepe with peach slices and top with sauce.

MAKES 16 CREPES

Acknowledgments

Our deepest heartfelt thanks to Sam Nassar for creating this opportunity. Without your idea, spark, and encouragement, this book would not exist. To the other four members of our cooking club, Carolyn Soriano, Lisa Frazzetta, Jessica Swartz, and Cindy LaCasse, we are so lucky to call each of you our friends. You are all incredible, classy women with hearts of pure gold. We are extraordinarily grateful to Susanne Nielson for her advice and guidance. Thanks to Peggy Frasse for introducing us to Sasquatch Books. Much gratitude and thanks to Terence Maikels and the amazing team of people at Sasquatch Books for your guidance, encouragement, and belief in our book from the very beginning. And finally, this book is bound by more than glue. It is held together by the unbreakable bond of friendship and created with the support, inspiration, honesty, sacrifice, hard work, laughter, and most of all the love we have for each other.

Dina Guillen

To my wonderful husband, Roland, for his love, support, and encouragement on not only this cookbook, but with every project I embark on. I love you with all my heart.

To my son, Andrew, who during the writing of this cookbook announced to me that he wanted to be a chef when he grows up so that he can make me proud: You are my life.

To my parents, Ghazi and Sylvia, who instilled in me from a very young age the love of food and cooking in a kitchen that was never off limits.

To my sister, Lamia, one of the best cooks I know: Some of my favorite moments on earth are spent in a kitchen with you, cooking, talking, and laughing.

A special thank you to my brother, Sam, who has the kindest heart and the most generous soul: You inspire me, you have taught me more than anyone about food and cuisine, and you make me so proud to be your sister. May all your dreams come true.

Michelle Lowrey

To my loving husband, Corey, my life didn't really start until we met, and there is no one I would rather spend my time with than you. Thank you for being my best friend and biggest fan.

To my hilariously funny children, Collin and Riley, you make me smile every day. I love being your mom.

To my wonderful parents, Sherry and Dennis, I thank you for being the inspiration for everything I do. You have given me everything I am. Your kindness and generosity of spirit knows no bounds. I love you both so very much.

Anna, you are in my heart forever. I will continue to work on the things you never got a chance to finish. Your strength, kindness, and hilarious wit sing all around me.

Maria Everly

To Farres Everly, my husband and partner. You have taught me the most about courage, faith, and kindness. You give me wings to find my dreams.

To my mother, Maria Hudson, for teaching me to take risks and giving me the belief that as long as you work hard, anything is possible.

To Julia Krieger and Nellie Hudson, you are the reason God created sisters. Julia, you are my angel and help me to be true to myself. Nellie, you keep me young and make me laugh. I love you all!

Gretchen Bernsdorff

To Mom, Dad, Katrina, and Grandma, thank you for truly being my biggest fans. Each of you believed in me, cried with me, and cheered me on through my greatest achievements and deepest heartaches.

To Ryan and Reed, you will always be in my heart for so many reasons. Thank you for eating every disaster and every masterpiece with equal enthusiasm. And thank you for bringing Maria to my life as a result of your friendship with Farres. She invited me into the cooking club and continually enriches my life.

To Kyle, my kindred spirit, thank you for always going the distance and I'll forever be smiling.

Index

About the Authors

DINA GUILLEN is a food junky and is hooked on the Food Network; she is always in the kitchen creating something unique. "You've got to try this" is her most commonly used phrase. Dina was a television talk-show host and producer for the CBS affiliate in Fresno before becoming vice president of a large public relations firm in the area. These days she spends her time working part-time developing marketing plans for various clients, and she is also a stay-at-home mom, making wonderful and creative meals for her husband and four-year-old son.

MICHELLE LOWREY loves to read cookbooks and is not embarrassed to admit that she reads them like fiction when she cannot sleep. She studied French pastry in San Francisco and worked at restaurants throughout the city. She currently stays at home with her two children, where the fanciest thing she does these days is cut the crusts off her kids' sandwiches. Her husband and children love her plank-grilling recipes, and she is very proud that the phrase "Mom, are you going to plank today?" is very common in her household.

Dina Guillen, Gretchen Bernsdorff, Michelle Lowrey, and Maria Everly

MARIA EVERLY is the eternal optimist of our group. She is just about the most bubbly and positive person you would ever want to know. An avid traveler, she has ventured throughout Mexico, Central America, the Caribbean, Europe, and the United States. While exploring each beautiful country, Maria takes in the gastronomic pleasures each place offers, from five-star restaurants to local hideaways, and from quaint cafes to open-air markets. Currently she is the area general manager for a finance company and she juggles her time between work, staying fit, remodeling her fifty-year-old home, her husband, and one very spoiled and loveable Labrador.

GRETCHEN BERNSDORFF is the dynamo of the group. By day she is a full-time analyst for a large mutual-fund company, and by night she is a full-time MBA student. Somewhere in that schedule, she fits in a running and weight-lifting regime that has brought her to the finish line of a couple of marathons. Her next goal is to conquer the triathlon. Where does that energy come from? Gretchen also goes the extra mile in the kitchen, where she has made low-fat yet scrumptious cooking a high art. While a healthy lifestyle is a top priority, she is known to eat her fair share of chocolate like the rest of us. (We love this about her.) And of course, come time for us to get together for our cooking club, she throws caution to the wind and eats . . . and eats.